Published in 1972 by Purnell
© 1972 by Purnell and Sons Ltd, London, W.1.
SBN 361 02030 9

Illustrations by Marion Mills

Edited by Christine McMullen

Maurice Burton's

WORLD OF NATURE

Purnell
London

Contents

Introduction

DR. MAURICE BURTON is a distinguished zoologist and author who has spent his life studying animals. He lives in Surrey and has kept many different animals ranging from tropical fish and a crocodile to a parrot, a genet and a family of foxes that live at the bottom of the garden.

This eighteenth century engraving of the dodo gives us a tantalising glimpse of a strange bird family now totally extinct.

In the last World of Nature we had much to say on conservation. As each year goes by the need for conservation grows greater. Also, more people are being made aware of this by what is said in broadcasts or written in newspapers. It is also being brought home to us in a practical way by what we see happening around us. In this book we have other examples of conservation although we are not making it our main theme. It is possible to over-do even a first-class subject by harping on it. So this year our central feature, or theme, is rather that of discovery.

This, in fact, cannot be divorced from conservation, as the article on the sea otter brings out. In this we point the moral that had the sea otter been exterminated, as at one time was feared, we would have lost a piece of information that is not only interesting in itself but is of value from a scientific point of view.

Those who preach the need for conserving animal species, such as the white rhinoceros, leopard, lion and so on, make the point that to the countries in which these are living they are a source of tourism. That is, they attract visitors.

Another reason the conservationists put forward for preserving our wildlife is 'that you cannot create a species'. By this they mean that if you wipe out a species no power on earth can bring it back. Since every species has its place in the natural scheme, each species. lost forever is like taking another brick out of a wall. The wall is weakened by just that little bit. At first no great harm is done but as one brick after another is removed the wall grows weaker. Continue doing this and the time must come when the wall will be in danger of collapse.

There is another side to this. By the time you have read this book I think you will realize—perhaps you already did—that there are many things we would like to know about animals but do not know. Every fresh discovery does not make us feel how much we know. It has the reverse effect. It makes us realize how much more there is to be learned, and how ignorant we are on many things.

We can compare scientific knowledge to putting together a jig-saw. We put a piece in there and a piece in here, and slowly the picture builds up. While doing a jig-saw there come tantalizing moments when we gaze at a gap and then search frantically among the remaining pieces to try to find something that will fit. Should some careless person have lost one or more pieces, or should some mischievous person have taken a few pieces away, we can never complete the picture.

This is exactly what happens when a species becomes extinct. It leaves a gap in our knowledge we can never fill. It may be only a small gap or it may be a large one. In the first instance we may be able to imagine what the whole picture would have looked like. In the second instance the gap may be so big we can never guess what should be in that corner of the picture.

For me, this is the strongest argument in favour of conservation, because we can never know what the next species studied will reveal to us. This, for me, is a stronger argument than preserving animals for tourism although I realize that the world being what it is, the tourism argument carries the most weight.

Think for a moment of some of the animals that have become extinct through man's action. There is the Tasmanian wolf which, if not actually extinct, is never seen. Then there is the passenger pigeon of North America, the quagga of South Africa, the dodo of Mauritius, and many others less well known. Suppose you had an Aladdin's lamp capable of wishing back an extinct species. Which of these would you like to see back?

I think I would go for the dodo. It was one of the strangest birds. Its name is from a Portuguese word meaning a fool. It must have looked quaint, and this alone would make it worth seeing in life. The fact that we should never have known what it looked like had not several people painted pictures of it in life is interesting. And the fact that they did so must have meant that it caught their attention more than usual.

Being such an odd bird its way of life must have been unlike that of almost any bird that has been alive during the last five hundred years, apart perhaps from the moas of New Zealand, which man has also killed off. It would be a fascinating game to try to imagine how the dodo lived. What sort of nest would it have built, what sort of eggs would it have laid, what would its chicks have been like? Unfortunately, guess as we will we can never know for certain. And apart from merely satisfying our curiosity, who knows, there may have been something about the dodo, about the way it was built, perhaps, that might have furnished an important clue to some problem or other in zoology that still perplexes us.

The dodo is not alone in this. We could say much the same of any other species that have been wiped out in the last thousand years. It would be a pity if fifty or a hundred years hence our descendants have to say: 'If only they,' that is, you and me, 'had not allowed the white rhinoceros, the leopard or some other animal, to become extinct. What valuable information we should have had, but which has been lost forever.'

Eels that Climb Walls

Have you ever seen an eel climb up a wall? Well, perhaps not. Have you ever seen one climb a steep bank? Or seen one crawl on land through the grass? Perhaps you have never seen an eel at all except in zoos or in a fishmonger's shop. The chances of doing so are small because as a rule eels lie in the mud at the bottom of the river or lake during the day and only rarely come to the surface.

I once saw one climb a steep bank, and this is something they must do quite often. As you know, our common eels start in the middle of the Atlantic and then swim, some to America and some to Europe, as larvae, and then change into young eels or elvers when they reach the coast. From there they make their way up the rivers and some even reach lakes. To get to the lakes they must crawl over the land and they must be able to climb over all sorts of obstacles.

I once read about eels in Australia having been seen climbing the almost vertical faces of rocky cliffs or climbing the concrete walls of water dams. They were said to keep on trying, often falling back into the water, until finally they reached the top of the dam.

To see eels climbing brick walls is a sight to be remembered. I was once on holiday staying at a mill house in Sussex. The old mill was no longer in use but the mill stream was still controlled by two sluice gates. The stream forked just before it reached the house and a branch went either side of it and each branch had a sluice gate. In front of one of them the water collected into a large pool before flowing through the meadows and I was told by somebody staying at the house that if I watched that pool in the evening I should see a sight which I would long remember.

The sluice gate itself was made of wood

Adult common European eels spend their lives in freshwater. When fully grown they return to the sea to spawn, making a three thousand mile journey to the Sargasso Sea to breed.

Eels take in oxygen through blood vessels in the skin and give out carbon dioxide in the same way, without needing their gills, when they are out of water. This means that they can travel overland from lakes and ponds if necessary on their return to the sea.

and it was set in a brick wall that rose vertically up from the water's surface. At the foot of the wooden sluice gate was a piece of sloping brickwork down which water was always trickling because the sluice gate was not completely watertight.

Nothing happened for a while but it was quite enjoyable sitting on the edge of the pool looking into its glassy surface and hearing little more than the trickle of the water from the sluice gate. Then an eel about a foot long surfaced in the middle of the pool and swam towards the brick wall. There it swam backwards and forwards along the brickwork as if trying to make out what it was. Then, as if having made up its mind that this was something it must climb, it swam back a short way then lunged at the brick wall half swimming, half jumping, and wriggled its way up several bricks before falling back into the water.

Then a larger eel appeared at the surface and it also swam at the brick wall. It managed to push its head into a hole between two of the bricks, then it wriggled

its tail backwards and forwards over the brick work as if seeking another hole higher up. There was none, but the tail was now wriggled over the brick work below where the head was wedged. It found a hole. The tail was pushed in, the eel pulled its head out of the other hole and stretched its body up full-length looking for another hold. Partly supported by its tail-hold and partly by pressing its body against the bricks it struggled to find another hold, but after a good deal of effort it fell back into the water.

By this time the surface of the pool was beginning to writhe with eels which one after the other tried to climb up the brick wall. In fact, the most surprising thing was that there were so many eels in that small pool. Each one in turn tried to get up the wall. Some fell, some got nearly to the top before dropping back into the water as they missed their next hold. A few of them managed to reach the brick slope in front of the sluice gate where there was this slight waterfall. One reached almost to the sluice gate, wedged its tail between two bricks and held it there for quite a long time while its body was lying in the water flowing down through the sluice gate.

Perhaps the best performance of all, certainly the most thrilling to watch, was by a medium-sized eel, which not only put its head in a hole between two bricks in the vertical wall but after a struggle disappeared entirely. After a while it reappeared, tail first, let its tail dangle for a while until it found another hole in the brickwork and again it disappeared inside the brickwork, this time tail first. Its acrobatic feat was not rewarded because when it came out of the brickwork the next time it fell back into the water and it had to start all over again.

Although I watched numbers of eels trying to climb the wall I did not see one of them get over it or over the sluice gate. Perhaps they did so later at night when it would have been difficult to see them even with a torch.

I did however go to the other sluice gate which also was made up of a brick wall with a wooden gate let into it, but this one was in such a position that it was possible to walk up the slight slope down which the water flowed, right up to the vertical brick wall, and there I could see some eels trying to climb.

I watched these for a while but all they were doing was clinging to the damp wall. They were hardly moving at all so it was not possible to see how they climbed this one but there was no doubt that they were climbing the wall. Several of them had reached different heights but the best of all was a small eel only $2\frac{1}{2}$ inches long and its body about $\frac{1}{8}$ inch thick and this had reached a height of 5 feet.

The eggs of eels are laid in mid-Atlantic. The larvae from them take a year to reach America and over two years to reach Europe. Once they have arrived at the coast they turn into elvers, or young eels. These swarm up the rivers. Some even go overland to lakes. The females go farthest up the rivers, the males staying nearer the coast. The mill stream where I saw the eels was not far inland. The eels may have been males or females but whatever they were they were striving desperately to go farther up the river.

Jane Burton

Large man-made obstructions do not deter eels. They will even climb walls to reach their freshwater home areas.

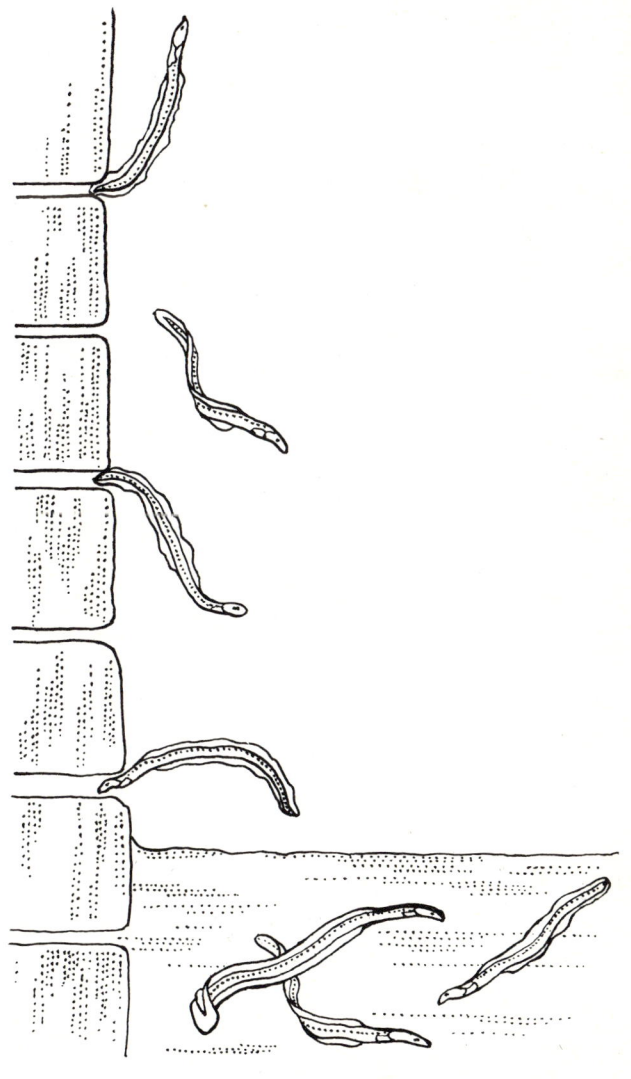

Animals Without any Colour

People often write to me saying they have seen a sparrow with white feathers in its wings, or perhaps they have seen a piebald blackbird or a pure white starling. One man wrote of seeing three birds flying together, a magpie with a crow on either side. When the birds landed he could see they were two black crows and a crow that was black with white patches. The people who write these letters always ask whether the white or partly white bird they have seen is rare. They are, of course, rare, and we call animals that are white, when they should be coloured, albinos.

There are, as we know, white animals which are not albinos. We think straight away of swans. Yet even these have some colour in their eyes, bill and feet. The colour in these parts are due to pigments. In most animals there is a great deal of pigment

This albino koala bear has pink eyes and muzzle because small blood vessel's show through its colourless, unpigmented skin.

Albino wallabies rarely survive in the wild as they are easily seen by their enemies, especially when they are young.

C M Jarman
C M Jarman

Bruce Coleman Ltd

A pure white blackbird is a very strange sight as it sits amid the green leaves of an oak tree. Albinism is fairly common among blackbirds and as it is hereditary the young of this albino blackbird may possibly be white or have white patches on their bodies.

giving a variety of colours. In a true albino the whole of the body lacks pigment, so the skin, hair, scales or feathers are white. The eyes are pink because there is no pigment in them and the blood in the blood-vessels lining the eyes shows through as pink.

White mice and white rats that we have as pets are true albinos. So is the ferret that is used for catching rabbits or for ferreting out rats. It is an albino polecat. These and others like them are true albinos. We sometimes see a pure white cat, but usually this does not have pink eyes, so it is not a true albino.

There are some animals that turn white in winter but they are not albinos. It is only the hairs in their winter coat, or the winter feathers as in the ptarmigan, that are white. There is still plenty of pigment in other parts of their bodies.

The name 'albino' was first given to Negroes of West Africa who had white patches of skin on their bodies. Then scientists adopted the word but changed its meaning. Zoologists used it for animals that had no pigment at all, that were white with pink eyes. Botanists used it for plants that had pale patches on their leaves, which we now call variegated. Animals that have only patches of white, like the crow, which looked like a magpie, we call partial albinos.

True albinism is inherited. At Olney, in the State of Illinois, in the United States, two albino grey squirrels were set free in 1905. Sixty years later there was a colony of them numbering 700. In Britain, where the North American grey squirrel was introduced, some albino grey squirrels were set free in Kent. Today, pure white grey squirrels can still be seen in Kent. Occasionally one is seen elsewhere in England but there are more white grey squirrels in Kent. They are descendants of those that were liberated.

Partial albinism can be inherited. The male European blackbird is a glossy black all over except for its orange bill. The hen is brown. Some years ago there was a male blackbird living in the centre of London that had a white throat. His offspring all had white somewhere on the body and for years there were partial albino blackbirds in that district. Then the albinism died out.

Partial albinism can also be due to a skin disease, and it can be caused by shock, at least in birds. It has been said it could be caused by the wrong food, but this is unlikely.

Probably the most famous animal albino was Moby Dick, the white whale in the story by Herman Melville. There is a white whale which is also known as a beluga. This one is dark grey when it is young. Later it becomes mottled, then yellow and loses all its pigment when it is four or five years old. Moby Dick was a killer whale, and killer whales are black with white patches. It just happened that Moby Dick was born with no pigment. A real life Moby Dick, a pure white killer whale was captured in 1971 and taken to the aquarium known as the whale pool at Sealand of the Pacific, in Victoria, British Columbia. It was a baby $12\frac{1}{2}$ feet long and weighing 1,500 pounds. A mile-long net costing 8 million dollars was needed to catch it and take it to Sealand. Then it was found to be a female, a 'Moby Doll'.

We talk of a white elephant as something that is useless. This is because an albino elephant is regarded by the peoples of south-east Asia as somewhat sacred and must not be made to work. Only wealthy people, such as kings, could afford to keep a white elephant because it cost so much to feed and could not be made to earn its keep. A white rhinoceros is something quite different. There are two rhinoceroses in Africa. One is called the black rhino, the other the white rhino, but both are grey, the first being a dark grey, the second a light grey. The reason why the second is called white is due to a mistake. The dark grey rhino has a hooked upper lip and is often called the hook-lipped rhino. The light grey rhino has a wide mouth and is often called the square-mouthed rhino. The Boers of South Africa called it *wyd*, meaning wide-mouthed. The British took this to mean 'white' and called it the white rhinoceros.

One of the nicest albinos was a baby loggerhead turtle, one of many seen making their way to the sea after hatching in the sand on the shore of South Africa. All were the usual colour except for one baby which was white tinged with pink.

Normally a peacock's train shimmers with shades of blue, bronze and green (see the display on page 45). Despite its lack of colour this albino peacock still struts proudly about, raising his train in an arc about his body and rattling his quills to attract peahens.

The Aces of the Air

Swifts are probably the finest bird aeronauts. Although only 7 inches long they have a wing-span of more than double this, and their wings are narrow and curved, like the blade of a scythe. They fly up to 68 m.p.h. or even more, although nobody has so far measured accurately their top speed. They spend the spring and summer in Europe and there they nest. In late summer they go back to Africa.

It has long been believed that swifts roost in the heavens. Now we know that they do spend the night on the wing, high in the sky. At dusk they can be seen flying up until they go out of sight and airmen have seen them at night, at heights of 10,000 feet, as if suspended in the air. A year ago, a scientist studying them in Africa found that there they never come to the ground at all. They are hunting flying insects all day and at night remain high in the sky.

Do swifts actually sleep on the wing? If so, how do they do it? Nobody knows. And think of the strain on their wings if they never rest them.

It has long been known that swifts drink on the wing. They fly down to water and just dip the lower part of the beak, scooping up the water. Then without stopping they fly up again. They bathe on the wing as well, either bathing when it rains or else flying down to the surface of a lake or river, dropping into the water and quickly flying up again. They shake the water out of their feathers with a quick trembling of the body, wings and tail as they fly.

We know that swifts mate on the wing but their nest is firmly positioned, in a tower or under a high roof. Before tall houses were built they nested in woodpecker holes in trees. They have only one family a year. The eggs take nearly 20 days to hatch and the

Arne Schmitz / Bruce Coleman Ltd

chicks are fed by the parents for six weeks after that. During this time the parents have to be constantly flying out to catch insects. They take turns on the nest, changing over every two hours, while incubating the eggs. So even while nesting each parent still spends half its time on the wing.

Unlike other birds, swifts can leave the eggs long enough for them to grow cold, yet they still hatch. They can leave their chicks to get cold or starve, if the weather is bad and flying insects are scarce. A baby chick can starve for days or weeks, where other chicks die in a few hours if left. The swift's chicks lose weight but make it up quickly when there is again plenty of food for them.

Birds must take great care of their feathers. Their lives depend on this. So they often preen the feathers to keep them in good condition. But they do so while perched or on the ground. We know swifts preen while they are on or near their nest. But do they preen while on the wing during the rest of the year? Nobody knows. The only clue we have is that sometimes they are seen scratching themselves in the air. When they do this they tumble like a pigeon but without losing height. So possibly they can preen in mid-air without falling to the ground.

Because they spend so long in the air, and because they fly so fast, swifts face a greater danger than most birds of having their eyes damaged by bits of debris in the air. So their eyes are set deep in the head and they have large, flexible lids as a further protection.

Swifts sometimes cling to a wall, especially when they are entering the nest. They have very short legs and weak toes, and it is often said that if they land on a flat surface they cannot take off again. This is not so. Several people have tested the birds for this. One even took off from a sheet of glass. They prefer, however, to keep on the wing.

As we watch swifts wheeling and weaving in the air, or playing in the air, as they often do, the marvel is they rarely collide, although they have been known to meet head on, and both birds be killed. Usually they brake hard and each flies vertically up,

Jane Burton

A swift's deep-set eyes have large flexible lids to protect them when flying at speed.

the two birds almost breast to breast.

With their skill as aviators accidents are few although cases of swifts flying into a brick wall and dying have been known. One hit a man's hat and was stunned. It is believed that the main cause of these accidents is that when a swift suddenly slows down to avoid a collision there is a rush of blood to its head. The swift hitting a soft hat suffered from this. Fighter pilots found that when suddenly increasing speed blood drained from the head and gave them a blackout. A sudden slowing down, on the other hand, can burst blood-vessels in the head, damaging the brain and even ending in death. To some extent the swift is protected from this. There are patches of thin bone in its skull so that it can expand when the blood rushes into the head, to ease the pressure. In most cases this special adaptation must be enough protection for the swift, the best aeronaut among the birds.

Spotted Peril for Greenfly

Ladybirds are favourites with us all. Even when we are children, before we learn there is such a word as 'insect', we find ourselves being told not to hurt a ladybird. When we grow up and start to grow roses we soon learn that these flowers have enemies. They are called greenfly, or aphides, or sometimes plant-lice. If the greenfly are there in plenty the leaves of the roses wither and the buds fail to open. One protection against this is to have lots of ladybirds around. Both as larvae and as full-grown insects they feed on greenfly, eating large numbers of them.

S C Bisserot / Bruce Coleman Ltd

A leaf-full of two-spot ladybirds. An adult has emerged, while others are in the pupal stage and one is still a larva.

Yet the ladybird was a favourite long before people knew how much they thinned the ranks of the greenfly and protected the flowers. Perhaps they were liked originally because they look so neat and so gay, in their red coats with black spots. But although these colours are pleasing to our eyes they have a more serious purpose for the ladybird.

Most animals are so coloured that they are not easy to see. Their colours form a camouflage, so protecting them from their enemies. There are a few creatures, and the ladybird is one, that flaunt their colours. They are bright colours which stand out usually red and black or yellow and black. We call them warning colours. Animals that wear these usually, if not always, have poison glands or a sting or have a nasty taste. So we say they are a warning, or sort of touch-me-if-you-dare.

Animals with warning colours make no attempt to hide, as if they knew they would not be molested. Somebody once went to the trouble of counting the numbers of insects fed by a pair of starlings to their young brood. The total was 17,000, of all kinds of insects, but only two were ladybirds although there were plenty about.

Other people have made the same sort of count and the results are always the same. There seems little doubt therefore that ladybirds, unlike most other insects, are seldom eaten by birds. This could be because they are not crowded together. Birds prefer not having to search hard for their food. We know that ladybirds are well spaced, or thin on the ground, as we say. Nevertheless, it is unlikely that that would explain the starlings taking only two in a total catch of 17,000, because ladybirds are so easy to see.

Most animals that prey on others live well spread out, it is the one way they can be sure of having enough to eat. Ladybirds only come together in winter or when they are migrating. The winter swarms are not often seen. Sometimes we find ladybirds hibernating in the house, but then they are in ones or twos, sometimes as many as half a dozen in a small space. More rarely they will gather in hundreds, even thousands under bark or in a porch. The explanation given for these is that by huddling together they keep slightly warmer than when they are scattered. Although they are cold-blooded their bodies do give out a slight heat and huddling preserves this. Yet a winter swarm may be on the top of a post, exposed to all weathers.

In California certain hilltops are habitually used as swarming places. There they are gathered and taken to fruit farms to feed on the insect pests. The next year their off-spring are back again hibernating in the same places.

The swarms seen migrating are even larger. Last year swarms were seen on the coast of Germany, around Hamburg, and two days later swarms were seen on the east coast of England. Many were lying dead in the grass on the cliff-tops while on the beach below, at the water's edge, a band of dead ladybirds 2 to 3 inches wide extended endlessly along the shore. The journey across the North Sea had been too much for many of them.

Since the 18th century at least there have been records of huge swarms of ladybirds flying from Europe to the English coast, from Newcastle in the north right down to Portsmouth on the south coast. In 1847, in Kent, the cliffs were swarming with them for three days. In 1872, one swarm over Yorkshire took three days to pass. In 1896, the streets of London were crowded with them. In 1952, a swarm passed across the coast of Suffolk and the dead alone, numbering millions, formed a red band on the shore extending for 40 miles.

The same kind of thing happens in other parts of Europe and elsewhere in the world. In 1939, near Alexandria, in Egypt, uncounted millions flew in from the sea and passed overhead. On the beach was a band of dead ladybirds a foot wide and 4–5 deep,

Jane Burton / Bruce Coleman Ltd

A brightly coloured African ladybird feeds on aphides. Ladybirds have large appetites and do a great deal of good by eating up huge numbers of these pests.

along 14 miles of the shore. A scientist who saw them estimated there were 4,500 million dead ladybirds alone, in addition to those that had flown overhead.

It is a puzzle why these, and other insects, should migrate long distances, as many of them do, never to return, and with many dying on the way. With ladybirds, at least, it is even more puzzling why having colours to protect them they should then throw away this advantage by long, suicidal journeys. What these journeys mean can be illustrated by an event on the Sussex coast in 1969.

Then, there was a procession, rather than a swarm, of cabbage white butterflies, ladybirds and hoverflies crossing the English Channel and landing on the English coast. Hoverflies, which often migrate with ladybirds, look like small bees or wasps and are the insect equivalent of helicopters. On this occasion the hoverflies settled on everything and everybody. Once they were settled they refused to move. You could not shake them off. You had literally to lift them off your hands or face, they were so tired with the journey.

Birds with Built in Thermometers

The first white men to travel through the regions where the mallee fowl live came home with stories of huge mounds 15 feet in diameter and 4 feet high. These were at first thought to be burial mounds made by the Aborigines and it is only just ten years since the full story has been told. It is a story of a bird that makes an incubator and uses its own thermometer to make it work properly.

The mallee fowl is about as large as a turkey. It makes a huge mound of sand and vegetable rubbish to use as an incubator. The incubator is needed because where the mallee fowl lives the nights in winter are freezing and those in summer are nearly so. The summer days, on the other hand, are very hot, as much as 100°F. So the usual kind of nest is not much use for the mallee fowl.

The female mallee fowl lays her eggs in the mound and after this the care of the eggs is taken over by the male. The heat of the sun is used but in a remarkable and deliberate manner, and so is the heat from the rotting vegetation. For eleven months of each year the male mallee fowl is occupied preparing and tending the nest. In May he and his mate together dig a large pit in the sand, scraping the earth out with their large and strong feet and legs. In June, which is the beginning of winter in Australia, they fill the pit with vegetable rubbish scratched together from a distance of anything up to 150 feet around the pit. They rake in dead leaves and stalks until the heap in the pit rises well above the level of the rim. Then it rains heavily, soaking the vegetable rubbish and making it heat up. In August the birds begin to mix sand with the decaying vegetation in a smaller pit at the centre of the mound. This is where the eggs will be laid and incubated.

Egg laying begins in September and by this time the mixture of sand and vegetation in the smaller pit has become quite warm. So it is opened up. The male tests the temperature and if he is satisfied that it is right, he makes way for the hen to lay her eggs. She also tests the temperature before laying, then scrapes away a small part of the mixture and lays an egg in the hole. The male now replaces the mixture in the smaller pit and scrapes the rest of the vegetable material over the mound.

Throughout September and the next three months the hen lays one egg after another, until there is a ring of eggs, each standing on end. As each egg is laid the two birds remove the top of the mould to lay bare the mixture in the smaller pit. Both test the temperature, and then the hen scratches a

The huge mound in the picture is built by the mallee fowl and his mate. Made of sand and decaying vegetation the mound is used as an incubator for the eggs.

The mallee fowl's egg chamber is scratched out of the main mound. The female lays the eggs but they are cared for by the male. He inspects the eggs frequently, digging them up to make sure they are at the right temperature. He uses his tongue to measure the warmth of the nest and then adds sand to cool it down or exposes the eggs to the heat of the sun.

hole in which to lay. When she has laid her egg the male again closes the incubator pit and replaces the leaves taken from the mound.

The hen lays her eggs at intervals of two days or more. During the intervals the mound is inspected daily, the male doing most of the work, to ensure that the temperature is correct. The hen may lay anything up to 33 eggs, each of which takes seven weeks to hatch. So by the time the last egg is laid chicks from the first eggs are already hatching. It also means that the last chicks will not leave the nest until February, or more usually, March. And all this time the mound is inspected daily and measures taken to ensure a correct temperature.

Should the mound show signs of becoming overheated, the mallee fowl simply opens it up to allow the excess heat to escape. If it shows signs of becoming too cool, the sun's heat is used to raise the temperature, the mound being opened up until the sun's rays fall directly onto the incubation chamber. At the same time, the materials that have been covering the chamber are spread around so that they can take in the greatest amount of heat from the sun before being put back over the eggs.

The temperature of air varies throughout each 24 hours and it fluctuates even more from one season to another. It is a remarkable feat therefore for the mallee fowl to keep the temperature of the nest steady all the time. In this, it uses its tongue and the inside of its mouth as a living thermometer. You can see the bird picking up a beakful of leaves from the mound, allowing them to touch the tongue and lining of the mouth. This tells it whether the inside of the mound is too hot, too cold, or just right.

23

Bounding Bouncers from Africa

It would not be surprising if you thought a springbok is a rugby footballer, because we hear so much about this famous South African rugby team. Other people also known as springboks were the South African soldiers who fought in the two World Wars.

In fact the real springbok is a kind of gazelle, noted for its jumping or springing. When a herd is startled they leap eight to ten feet into the air in spectacular stiff-legged jumps before bounding off at top speed. This was what gave the springbok its name.

In the 17th century, the Dutch East India Company founded a provisioning station at the Cape of Good Hope. The officials running the station gave Dutch names to the vast herds of antelopes they saw. In Dutch a buck is 'bok' and the most numerous antelopes in the countryside around were the jumping bucks or springboks. These early South African settlers were so impressed with the springboks they took them as their national emblem.

We know there were vast herds of springboks because some of the people living in South Africa in the 19th century wrote down their impressions of them, and especially of their migrations. In certain years millions of springboks would trek across country in vast columns. Gordon Cummings was one who wrote about them. He said: 'I beheld the boundless plains and even the hillsides, which stretched away on either side, thickly covered not with herds but with one vast mass of springbucks: as far as the eye could strain the landscape was alive with them.'

He wrote this after seeing the last great trek, in 1896. Today, in South Africa, springboks are found mainly on farms, and a farmer owning 50 or 100 of them is proud of the

fact. There are a few more in Southwest Africa, but even there the most that are seen at one time, when they mass together, is 80 or 90 thousand—nothing to the millions there used to be.

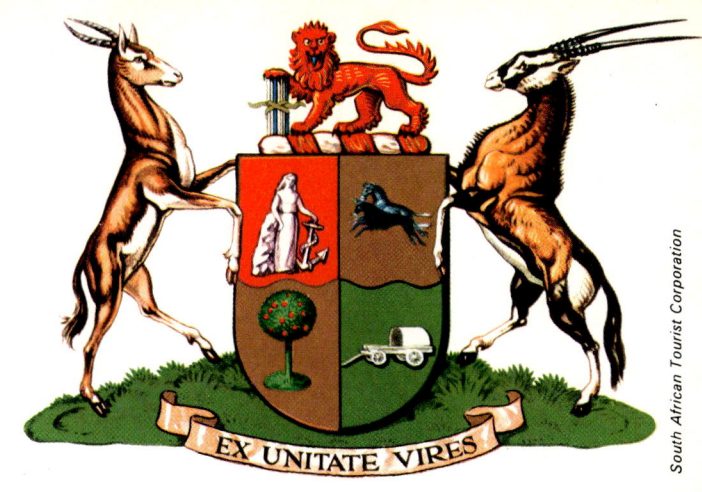

Right. The springbok is proudly featured on the South African national emblem (Left).
Below. When frightened springboks may leap high in the air in terrific bounds.

South African Tourist Corporation

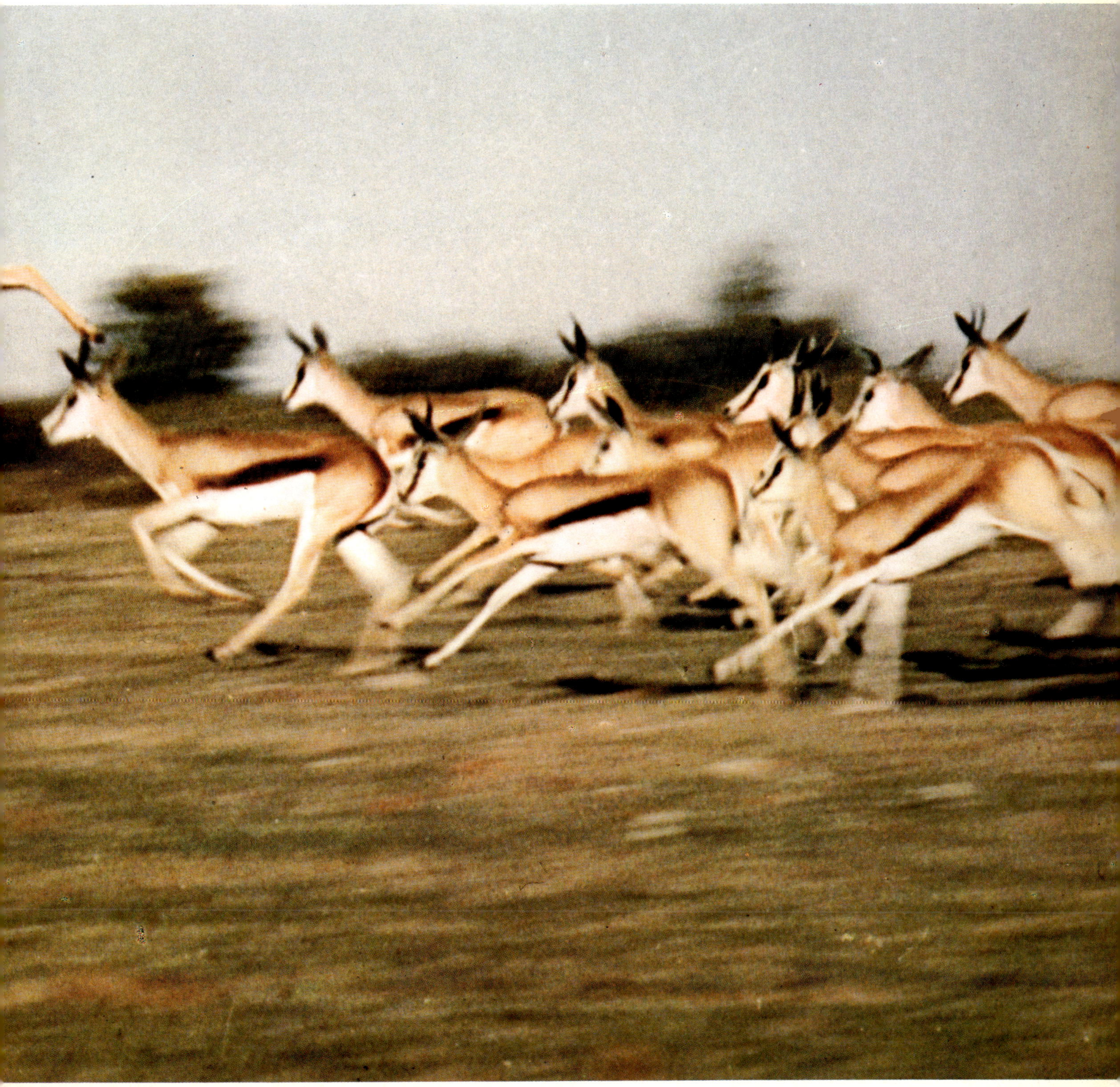

Some of the things that were written about them then help us to get an idea what an incredible sight it must have been. 'The whole country seemed to move', wrote one man, 'in one continuous stream, on the road and both sides of the road, to the skyline.' He drove through the swarm and the plodding springboks just moved aside enough to avoid the wheels of his cart.

A swarm would take 24 hours to pass and might cover an area 138 miles in one direction and 15 miles in the other. When the leading springboks came to a river they were pushed into the water by the press from behind and drowned. More and more were drowned until the rest of the swarm were able to cross on the bridge formed by their bodies, we are told.

The springboks were killed by the flesh-eaters, such as the lions. Many became diseased or died from other causes. There are even stories that when they reached the sea the leading animals were pushed forward by the weight of those behind and drowned.

Now, seventy years after the last great trek, scientists are trying to piece together why the treks took place, and why the springboks have almost disappeared.

Not all the springboks migrated. Some stayed behind. It was merely the surplus numbers that went, apparently in search of fresh pastures. Even those that stayed moved about to some extent. It seems springboks can smell rain a long way off, and in the semi-desert areas where they live rain means fresh vegetation. Even today, in Southwest Africa, they still move into areas where it is raining. The Bushmen who live there say the springboks follow the thunder and lightning.

Just before a trek started groups of springboks would start moving about restlessly. They would gather aimlessly in mobs, uneasy as if their nerves were on edge. The slightest sound would make them scatter in all directions, and any unusual sight or sound would make them turn back or drive them off in one direction. Finally, the assembled swarm would move off.

One explanation given for this apparently aimless trek was that although spring-boks can go without drinking, getting the water they need from succulent vegetation, every two or three years they became afflicted with thirst. Then they set off in search of water, and would drink even salt water.

Whatever the truth of this, it is certain that the migrating springboks suffered badly, once their native land was being used for farming. To begin with their millions of hoofs cut the ground to pieces wherever they went and trampled the vegetation. Where crops had been planted this meant ruin to the farmers. So, when the springboks began to move the Dutch farmers went out in their hundreds to shoot them. There was a further reason why the farmers should do this. They could sell the hide of a springbok for sixpence and the meat for two shillings. The meat was dried and was then known as biltong.

Even although the farmers shot the springboks by the hundred, this could not have made much difference to the swarms of millions. Perhaps it was the disease known as the rinderpest, that swept Africa in the early years of this century, which really put an end to the migrations, in addition to the land being taken over for farming.

We shall never again see the spectacular sight of so many springboks migrating. We shall probably never know for certain why they migrated in this way or what happened to them at the end of the migration.

It is interesting if unpleasant to note that the sad story of the springbok is similar to that of many animals which have been chosen as national emblems. Several countries adopted the eagle and eagles everywhere have been persecuted and are in danger of dying out. The bald eagle of the United States, for example, is in real danger of extinction. The emu, one of Australia's emblems, is still plentiful but is apt to be shot at when it goes onto farmland. The kiwi of New Zealand, for other reasons, is becoming scarce.

In the case of the springbok we can end on a happier note as its decline seems to have been halted and now, although numbers are very low, the springbok population in South Africa is beginning to increase.

Farming Crocodiles Instead of Cattle

There were crocodiles living in rivers 150 million years ago when the giant dinosaurs were first around. In fact, crocodiles are related to dinosaurs. At that time there were crocodiles of all sizes, some less than seven feet long and others 50 feet long, nearly twice the size of the largest living today. Big crocodiles are very rare today because some years ago somebody discovered that the skin of a crocodile makes good leather. A fashion set in for having things made of crocodile skin. High prices were paid and the bigger the skin the higher the price it would fetch in the markets. The men who went out shooting the crocodiles did not waste their time on the small ones, they shot the big ones.

Very soon it was hard to find a big crocodile, so they shot the medium-sized ones. Then these became scarce and the hunters were glad to shoot even the smaller ones. There were stories of hunters, when told there was a small crocodile somewhere, going to the expense of hiring a plane to go and shoot it. Whether true or not, such stories show the great demand for crocodile leather and the high prices paid for it.

Most people think of crocodiles as savage killers and probably feel, if they stop to think about it at all, they would be better out of the way. They would be surprised, no doubt, to learn that crocodiles can be important to fisheries.

About the time that crocodile leather was first in such demand an important research was carried out that showed crocodiles do not eat as much fish as the fishermen claimed. In fact, in some ways, crocodiles help to preserve fish.

This is because baby crocodiles feed only on insects and as they grow older the number of insects they eat decreases and they turn to other freshwater animals such as crabs, spiders and water snails. Medium sized crocodiles do eat fish although when fully grown they catch water birds and eat animals that come to the waterside to drink.

So it is only the medium sized crocodiles that eat large numbers of fish and not the whole population. Many of the fish these medium-sized crocodiles do eat are in fact the fish-eating fish and so by removing these the crocodile helps the human fisherman to obtain a good catch.

You might say that a few crocodiles are all right but left alone there might be too many of them. That is unlikely. Large crocodiles are apt to eat the baby crocodiles or even those that are larger than babies. When the sun is hot crocodiles come out on land to bask and in any sunbathing group the crocodiles are all much the same size. The tiny ones keep together, so do the small ones and those of medium size, and all keep well away from the large ones. This is one way of avoiding being eaten by other crocodiles. They cannot keep in size groups all the time and often small crocodiles are eaten by those larger than themselves.

Young crocodiles like this one from the Nile feed on small crabs and water snails.

Jane Burton

These crocodiles are being reared on a special crocodile farm in Africa. When fully grown their skins may be sold to make expensive leather handbags.

Crocodiles also play an important part as scavengers. For a good example of this we can turn to the hippopotamuses. Male hippos sometimes fight in the water, each trying to break a leg of its opponent. They inflict severe wounds on each other but these usually soon heal. A broken leg, however, means certain death because a hippo, with its great weight, cannot walk on land to its feeding ground, among the tall grasses. A dead hippo rotting in water would soon make the water foul. Vultures cannot feed on it very easily, nor can jackals and hyenas. Crocodiles do. They take large lumps out of it by seizing them between their jaws then making a quick roll with their whole body. This twists and wrenches the flesh away.

Other large animals sometimes meet their death in water, such as elephants and buffaloes. Where there are crocodiles their carcases are cleaned up.

The crocodile's fearful reputation as a killer may be exaggerated. Many African women live near a river or a lake, where there are crocodiles. They have to go to the water's edge to draw water or wash clothes. If one of the women is seized by a crocodile, pulled into the river and drowned then the crocodiles get a bad name. They are treated as vermin.

Surprisingly, in some places crocodiles are not a danger to human beings although in other places they are. Why this should be is not known for certain. In some parts of West Africa, for example, wooden palisades are erected to protect the women going down to draw water. When a female crocodile is guarding her nest or her young ones she can be dangerous. It seems also that in those places where the streams and pools in which they live dry up, so that the crocodiles cannot easily escape, they are apt to be bad tempered and to snap at people.

There may be other causes. In Lake Kariba a man was spear-fishing when a crocodile seized his foot. He was wearing frogman's flippers on his feet and probably the crocodile mistook the flipper for the tail of a large fish. The man lost his flipper but escaped with nothing worse than some large toothmarks in his foot.

In spite of these drawbacks there has been growing anxiety that crocodiles, which managed to outlive their relatives, the dinosaurs, might become extinct. Already 14 out of the 21 existing species are seriously threatened with extinction. The Cuban crocodile, for example, was hunted for its leather until, in 1965, there were only 500 left. These were mainly young ones, in the Zapata Swamp, an area of not much over half a square mile. There may have been a few more elsewhere than in the swamp. The Cuban crocodile is found nowhere else in the world than in Cuba and the nearby Isle of Pines, so the Cuban government passed laws protecting this crocodile.

In parts of Africa it is now realized that people want to see crocodiles when they come as visitors. They are a tourist attraction, and tourists bring money into the country. Moreover, if crocodile skins mean money to hunters there is no reason why crocodiles should not be looked after and used for this purpose, almost like domestic cattle. In one place in Africa a hatchery has been started. There the baby crocodiles are fed and tended until large enough to be set free in the rivers. It is the beginning of crocodile farming, which may mean that eventually there will be enough crocodiles to provide leather for handbags as well as excitement for tourists without destroying the many wild species.

Huberta the Explorer Hippo

Most of us when we grow up want to have a home of our own, preferably with a garden, and settle down, as we say. There are some people, however, that like to wander. We say they have itchy feet. Some become explorers, some drift from one job to another and some take to the roads. We used to call these last people tramps because they were always walking from place to place, tramping the roads and never settling down. Only within the last few years has it been fully realized that animals show this same pattern.

Normal hippopotamuses stay close to the main herd and spend their days in the river, only leaving the water to graze.

'Mud, mud, glorious mud, Nothing quite like it for cooling the blood . . .' hippopotamuses are extremely fond of wallowing in mud. They make huge hollows at the sides of the river banks and make frequent visits to lie down in the soft, sticky earth. Besides helping to keep the hippos cool during the day the mud probably removes insects and irritating parasites that have burrowed down into the hippopotamuses' hide.

One of the modern methods of studying animals is to live-trap them and mark them in order to keep a watch on their wanderings. This is especially true of small animals such as mice and shrews, weasels and others of similar size. As a result of these studies we know that the great majority of animals occupy what is called a home range. That is to say, they have a nest, den or lair and they do not wander very far from this. They are the home lovers. The larger the animal the larger its home range is going to be but even when the home range is large there are definite boundaries to it and the animals keep within these boundaries. Then the people that were live-trapping these animals found that every now and then their traps caught one that had not been in that home range before. It began to dawn on them that there are a few animals in each

29

species that have itchy feet, like the people who cannot settle down. They call these wanderers transients, meaning animals that are only passing through.

Years ago people climbing Mount Kenya, which is 14,800 feet high found the body of a leopard right at the top preserved in ice on the snow-capped peak. The puzzle was why the leopard should be up there when it is really an animal of the East African plains. A few years after this on Mount Kadam in Uganda somebody climbing the mountain saw a black-and-white colobus monkey sitting on a pile of stones right at the top of the mountain at a height of 10,050 feet. The real home of this colobus monkey is down on the lower slopes. What the leopard was doing on Mount Kenya and the monkey on Mount Kadam is hard to say, but it could easily be that these were two animals with itchy feet. It just happened that one of them died on the summit and its body was preserved in ice and the other one was seen by chance by somebody climbing the mountain, otherwise we should not have known that they had done so. It is very

likely that other animals have done the same sort of thing and have not been noticed. There was, for example, the time when somebody saw bear tracks going up the side of a mountain in Canada. He followed them and found they went right to the top of the mountain. Then, down the other side, he could see the track where the bear had tobogganed down, either on its back or on its belly. This seems to be another instance of an animal that loved to wander.

Lieutenant-Colonel J. H. Williams (Elephant Bill) tells in a book of a young elephant belonging to the South Andaman Forest Department that went off on a jaunt that lasted for 12 years. It was a seven-year-old calf when it took itself off and it moved from island to island in the Andaman's group of islands, in the Indian Ocean, and was last seen 200 miles from its starting point. It had swum from one island to another. In some places the islands are a mile apart and there is always a heavy swell on the water so it was quite a remarkable feat. Colonel Williams does not tell us what happened eventually to this elephant.

The most extraordinary story of an animal's wandering is of a hippopotamus. As we know, hippopotamuses spend most of their time in the water or resting on the bank. At night they go on land to feed. Each hippopotamus follows a particular path, wandering into the long grass and feeding. Each keeps to its own territory, and having fed it wanders back to the river. In 1928 a hippopotamus was born in the water of St. Lucia Bay in Zululand. When it was old enough to walk about on its own it headed south-west and during the next three years it just tramped steadily on for a distance of 550 miles, as the crow flies. In a very short time this hippopotamus had become famous. The people of South Africa began to take notice of it and they called it Huberta.

People began to watch for Huberta and her wanderings were recorded in local papers all along the route, so we have a complete record of her journey and the times that she appeared near the various towns on the way. The people of South Africa not only watched Huberta as she passed through their particular town or

Scale in miles (approx)

Huberta born here

St Lucia Bay

Here Huberta lived and then began her wandering. October 1928

Stanger

Pietermaritzburg

Durban

Port Shepstone

St John

INDIAN OCEAN

King Williams Town

East London

Here Huberta was killed 1931

It is so hot in the African sun that hippopotamuses spend as much time as possible in the water. Their nostrils and eyes protrude so that they can lie almost completely submerged in the water for hours at a time to keep out of the heat.

village but they developed quite an affection for her and took an interest in what was happening to her. So much so that Huberta became a sort of national pet and one that everyone wanted to protect. Unfortunately Huberta came to a sad end. A trigger-happy man who had not heard about her journey, or if he had, did not realize that this was the famous hippopotamus, saw her bathing in a river where hippopotamuses rarely occurred and shot her. Only when she was dead was it found that 'she' was a male. Her skull and her hide are preserved in the museum at Williamstown in Natal, South Africa.

We shall never know why Hubert, as we must call the hippopotamus now, made this extraordinary journey. It may even be that this kind of wandering happens more often than we think. It could be that many other animals of every species have wandered in this same way unnoticed. It could even be that this is the way animal species become spread over the earth, by some of their more adventurous members, like Hubert, just wandering off and keeping going.

From St. Lucia Bay to Williamstown Hubert had to cross at least nine large rivers and probably other smaller ones as well. In those days there were many colonies of hippopotamuses in this part of Africa although today they may be many fewer. Hubert must have passed very close to many of these colonies. We can imagine the hippopotamus meeting others of its own kind all the way along the route and yet it kept steadily on, a solid, solitary figure plodding to an unknown destination.

Apart from the interest of the long journey there is a moral here which has much to do with the present efforts so many people are making to protect animal species. It is this. It took a lot of people to protect Hubert: it took only one to kill him. That is why it is so important in conservation to win over as many people as possible rather than rely on the efforts of a few enthusiasts.

A Plant that Man Cannot Control

Bracken is so beautiful that we never think of it as a plant pest. In the early part of the year it pushes up its coiled leaves which then expand to give the beautiful flimsy fronds that later in the year turn a mellow brown. Without it many of our hillsides and heaths would lack their most charming features. Yet bracken is so dense that it shades the ground beneath and little can grow under it. It is so vigorous that it can readily invade good agricultural land and is then very hard to destroy. It can be used as litter for pigs and cattle and if properly treated as fertilizer but such uses have rather gone out of fashion today because of the cost of cutting and carting the bracken.

One of the surprising things about bracken is that it is so widespread. It can be found over the whole of Europe and most of Asia and in North and Central America, from the Arctic Circle to the tropics. Bracken is a fern and ferns were growing on the Earth before ever flowering plants came into existence. They flourished most 300 million years ago at the time when our coal was first being laid down in the form of dead vegetation. These very early ferns died out as the millions of years rolled by and other kinds took their places, but of all of them there is none to compare with the bracken for the wide area it occupies over the Northern Hemisphere.

There are two reasons for this. The first is that the bracken grows horizontally instead of vertically as do the other plants with which we are more familiar. That is to say, it has an underground stem which grows parallel with the surface of the ground, pushing out branches as it grows. The fern fronds themselves are the leaves that arise from these branches. So, unseen, the bracken can push its branches into land that could otherwise be made to bear crops, and once it has done so only the most determined battle will defeat it.

Another reason why bracken is hard to get rid of is that cattle and horses do not eat it because it is poisonous to them. Sheep usually leave it well alone, too, but in 1954 bracken began to disappear from large stretches of hill country in Wales. Scientists began to get excited about this. They thought it might be a new disease that was

Jane Burton/Bruce Coleman Ltd

Young bracken fronds push up through the soil early in the spring. Gradually the closely packed delicately coloured new bracken unfurls into an adult plant. The fern will be fully expanded by June or July and may be from one to six feet tall.

Right. The adult bracken plant.

killing off the bracken. Had this been so it would have meant they had a new weapon with which to fight the troublesome fern. Then it was found that sheep in the area were not only eating the bracken but eating it with relish, instead of just nibbling a piece of the fern here and there. The farmer who owned the sheep could hardly believe his eyes as bracken is not usually popular with sheep although it is not poisonous to them.

The third reason why it is so widespread is because of the large number of spores it produces. Being a fern it does not bear seeds formed in flowers but has spores borne directly on the leaves. These are in very small capsules packed in their tens of thousands under the rolled up edges of the leaflets of the frond. In summer we can turn

33

over a frond and see these packed capsules as a brown margin on the underside of the bracken. When the spores are ripe the capsules burst and the spores, so minute that we cannot see them except with a magnifying glass, float in the air. They are lighter than the lightest dust, so light that even a gentle wind will carry them up into the air and carry them long distances. Each spore is less than 1/2000th of an inch in diameter.

I once tried to count the number of spores on a single bracken frond. We were picnicking in a wood on a hot summer's day, in the sort of weather when it is a great pleasure to sit and do nothing except enjoy the scenery. The thought occurred to me to count the bracken spores. I broke off a leaflet and with my hand lens examined several of the capsules and counted the spores in each one. This gave me an average for the number of spores per capsule. I then counted the number of capsules on this leaflet and then counted the leaflets on a well-grown frond. By simple multiplication I arrived at the staggering figure of 27 million spores on a single bracken frond. I did not attempt to count the number of fronds in that one wood, but if I had done so the number of bracken spores that were going to be liberated even in that small wood would have run into countless billions.

Now we can see why whenever a sample of air is taken, as meteorologists do in order to test the pollution of the atmosphere, one of the things likely to be in the sample is bracken spores. They float high up in the air kept aloft by the winds and carried across continents and seas, even over mid-Atlantic. Sooner or later they will fall to the earth and provided they fall on damp ground there is a reasonable chance that they will give rise to new bracken plants sometimes in quite unexpected places. Given suitable conditions we find it springing up among bricks and mortar even in the hearts of big towns such as the centre of London, far from the countryside. The wastage of spores, however, must be tremendous. If it were not so the northern continents would soon be covered by nothing else but bracken.

The little foal is a recent addition to the herds of wild ponies in the New Forest. Although the ponies keep the grass cropped very short they leave the huge areas of bracken severely alone as it is poisonous to them and to cattle.

Jane Burton / Bruce Coleman Ltd

Picture Puzzle:

Can you identify these strange shapes?

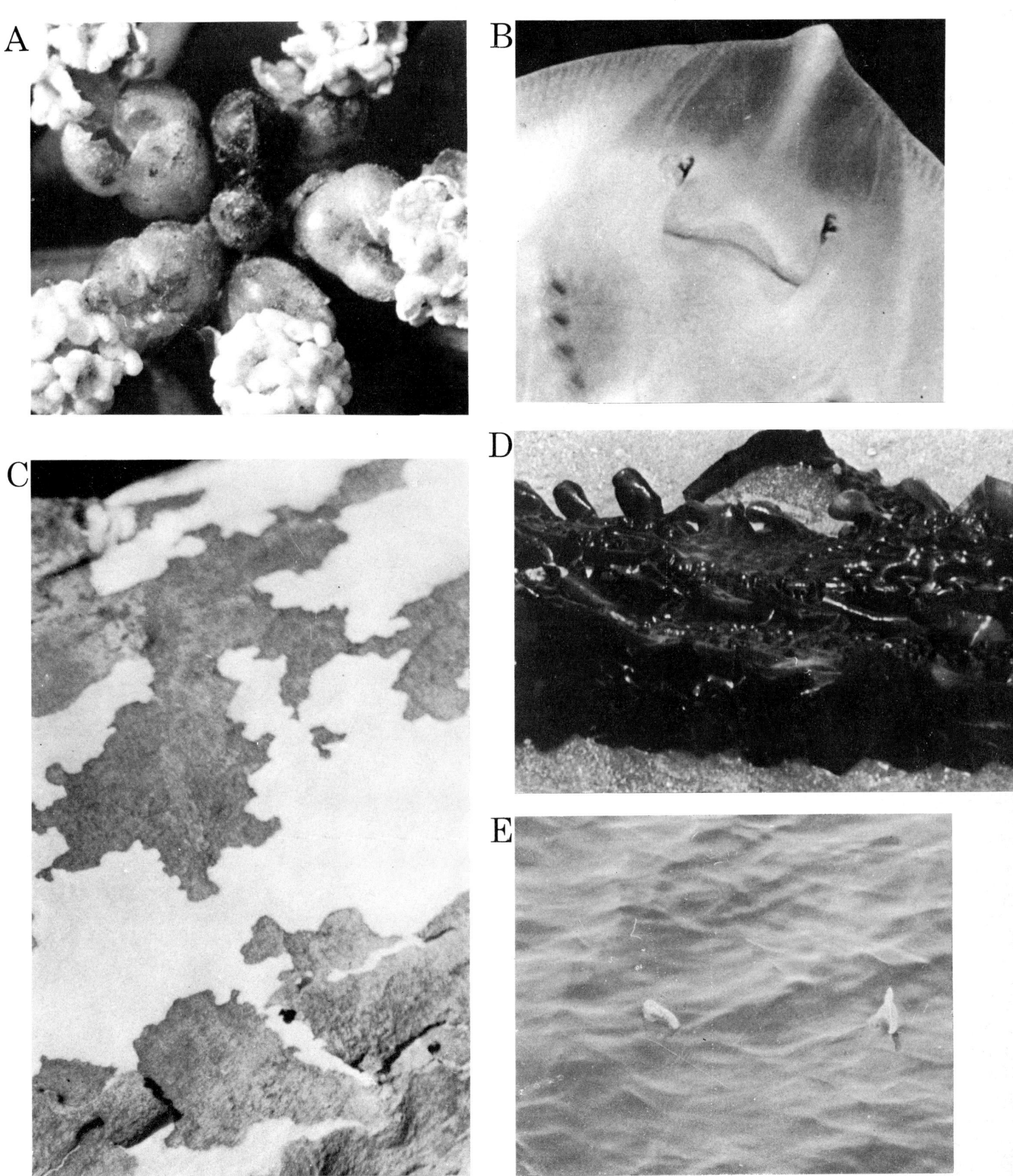

A

B

C

D

E

Now turn to page 92 to check your answers.

A Leaf-Eater Among the Whales

There is no real difference between whales, dolphins and porpoises. As a rule, the smaller kinds of whales are called dolphins and porpoises and the larger ones are called whales. Even this rough rule breaks down in practice because some of the small whales are still called whales. Zoologists solve this knotty problem by calling them all cetaceans, from the Latin word *cetus* meaning a whale.

We cannot be sure which land animals cetaceans are most closely related to but it seems likely their nearest relatives are cattle and antelopes. Should this be correct then the distant ancestors of whales were vegetarians. If so, they have changed their diet since they left the land to live in the sea.

Of the 92 species of cetaceans a few are known as whalebone whales, such as the right whale. These have teeth in their gums before they are born but they never break out. Instead, horny plates grow down from the roof of the mouth. These baleen plates, as they are called, are set closely together to form a sieve on either side of the mouth. When feeding, a whalebone whale opens its mouth to take in a huge quantity of water filled with a kind of shrimp, known to the whalers as krill. The whale then closes its mouth. The water is forced out at the sides and the krill is left behind on the inner side of the baleen plates. It is then swallowed.

The rest of the cetaceans, that is, 81 of them, such as the sperm whale, feed on fishes, octopuses, squids and cuttlefishes. A few eat lobsters, crabs and shrimps as well. The one exception is the killer whale, which eats porpoises and seals and, working in packs, will even attack large whales. Killer whales will eat almost any kind of meat.

In brief, therefore, whales are flesh-eaters, certainly eaters of animal food. It was with some surprise therefore that scientists studying the carcase of a dead dolphin stranded on the banks of the Kamerun river, West Africa, found its stomach was filled with leaves, mangrove fruit and grass. It became famous as the only vegetarian whale, and was also looked upon as a very rare species because only this one specimen had ever been seen. Then, in 1958 and 1959, two French scientists exploring the rivers in Senegal found that the West African white dolphin, as it was called, was anything but rare. They saw several of these

The gigantic sperm whale may reach lengths of over seventy feet. To nourish its huge body it feeds on vast quantities of squid which it catches in its massive, toothed jaws.

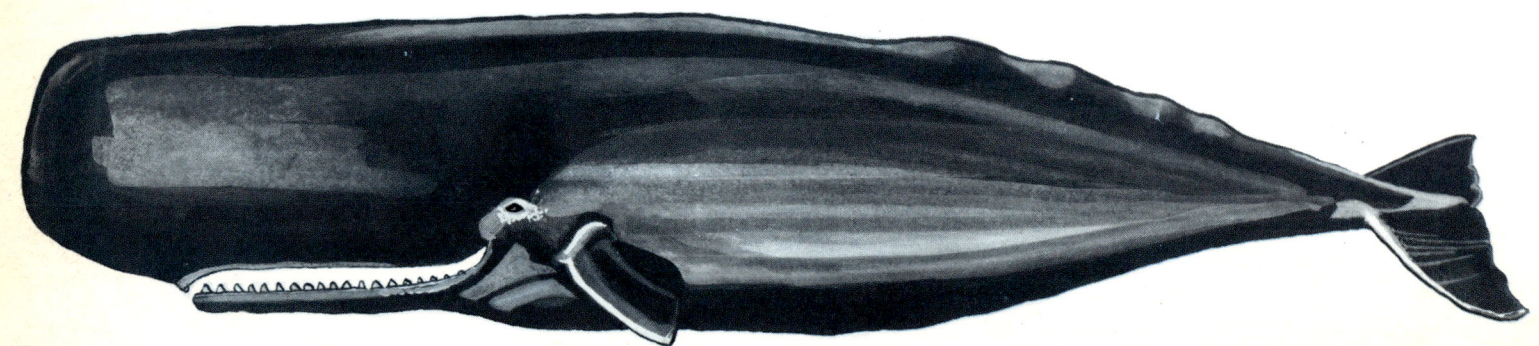

Killer whales are extremely dangerous predators. They hunt in packs and catch smaller whales, such as dolphins and porpoises.

Below. The Gangese dolphin lives in fresh or brackish waters of estuaries and rivers.

dolphins every day, especially at low tide, during the period January to April. They also learned that they ate nothing but fish.

This leaves us with a first-class mystery, why this one dolphin should have had its stomach filled with vegetable food. The only explanation so far put forward is that the leaves, fruit and grass must have been in the stomachs of the fishes it ate. The dolphins studied in the Senegal rivers ate mainly mullets and similar fishes that feed either on very small algae or on small aquatic animals.

The West African white dolphin is only seven feet long. The fishes it eats are seldom more than a foot long. They are hardly the kind of fishes to swallow quantities of leaves, fruits and grass. But if these plant materials did not come from the stomachs of the fishes it ate, we can only suppose the dolphin picked them up itself from the water. If so, why should it do this. There is as yet no explanation that will hold water.

The Greenland Right whale feeds on tiny shrimps called krill. These are sieved out from the sea in their thousands by the huge baleen plates between the whalebone jaws.

Population Explosion in the Starling Family

Which would you say is the most numerous bird in the world? My guess would be the common or European starling. Certainly this is the most widespread bird today. Yet 200 years ago, so we are told, starlings were so rare that they were caught and kept in cages as pets. Nobody would think of doing so today, not because the bird lacks interest for us or is unattractive to look at, but because it is so common in our gardens. Its plumage in summer is a rich mixture of colours, especially when the glancing rays of the sun light up its feathers. It has a fluty whistle not unpleasing to the ear, but above all it is a remarkable mimic of all kinds of sounds including the songs of other birds.

By the beginning of the 19th century starlings were becoming common in England but were still rare in Scotland, where people were still buying them for pets. So although we do not have exact figures to prove the point, it looks as though 200 years ago starlings were becoming more numerous and were spreading. It seems to have been the same in other parts of Europe. We know, for example, that they have spread northwards in Scandinavia and from there onto some of the islands in the Arctic Ocean. More recently, and this we can be sure of, the first starlings reached Iceland, in 1930. At first they did not breed, those already there being merely joined by fresh starlings coming over from Europe. Then, in 1941 the first pairs were seen nesting.

Starlings conquered new territory in Europe and adjacent lands on their own but they have been taken by man all over the world, where they have settled and flourished. In 1861 some starlings were taken to Victoria, Australia. These became popular as pets and more were taken in the following years. They were allowed to fly free. At first

Each evening huge flocks of starlings swarm into cities to roost. In Trafalgar Square they perch on every tiny ledge, their droppings fouling the buildings.

Jane Burton

they did not breed. When they did their numbers began to increase rapidly and before long they spread northwards into New South Wales and later into Queensland. They also spread southwards into Tasmania and westwards into South Australia. Today they are so numerous in these regions that they have become pests in the fruit-growing districts of Australia where they can often be seen in vast flocks.

Starlings were also taken to New Zealand, to Hawaii and to South Africa. In all these places they have flourished, increased in numbers and become something of a nuisance.

The most spectacular spread has, however, been in North America. Between 1870 and 1900 more than a dozen attempts were made to introduce starlings into the United States and Canada. All but one of these failed because the birds did not breed and died out. Then, in 1890, 60 starlings were released into Central Park in New York, and 40 more were released the following year.

For the first few years the starlings stayed in the Central Park. As their numbers began to increase they began to wander, especially in autumn and winter, and by 1900 they had spread over most of the New England States. In the next 10 years they began to spread westwards. By the 1930s they had reached the Middle West, and they had pushed out northwards into southern Canada and southwards into Florida. In the early 1940s the first starlings crossed the Rocky Mountains into California and by 1949 they had reached the Pacific coast.

Even in the 1920s people in the United States were becoming alarmed at the spread of the starlings and by their large numbers. Scientists were asked to look into the matter to see what harm the starlings might be doing. In 1929 they reported that starlings were a nuisance because of the way they ate cherries, apples, corn and other crops and because of their roosting habits. Outside towns starlings roost in trees in large numbers and sometimes their droppings foul the ground killing off the plants below. But scientists also reported that the starling

Starlings may lay from 4–9 pale blue eggs. The ugly chicks are fed by their parents for the first three weeks of life. By then, like the fledgling starling below, they have developed brown plumage which does not change to the glossy blackish colour of the adult until the next year.

Jane Burton / Bruce Coleman Ltd

Starlings as a family are found all over the world. This splendid Superb Glossy Starling comes from southern Africa.

was probably the most valuable insect eater because it fed on insect grubs in the ground and in the trees, in surprising quantities, and some of these grubs are among the worst pests on farmland.

Perhaps the biggest nuisance of all, the American scientists reported, was the one people had begun to complain about in Britain. This was due to a rather surprising change in the starling's habits.

Up to the time that the first starlings were taken to New York, the birds were fairly common in the parks in London, but although they spent the day in the parks feeding they flew out into the countryside in the evening to roost. Then in 1894 it was noticed that starlings were staying in London, and others were coming in each evening, to roost. At first they roosted in the trees in the parks. Then suddenly Londoners became aware that large numbers of starlings were roosting on the buildings in the centre of London. By 1922 there was a huge dormitory stretching from Trafalgar Square to St Paul's Cathedral where tens of thousands of starlings came each night to roost, on the ledges and windowsills of large buildings as well as private houses.

London was not alone in this. In all big towns, and in small ones, too, starlings flew in towards evening to gather in their thousands on tall buildings.

Strangely enough the same thing was happening in the United States. It is not unexpected that starlings should roost on buildings because their ancestors were cliff-dwellers and roosted on cliff ledges. The surprise is that they should have suddenly changed from roosting in the trees to going back to their ancestral habits of roosting on ledges. And it is even more surprising the starlings in the United States should have also started to do so about the same time.

Since this habit first developed starlings have become such a nuisance everywhere that all kinds of tricks have been tried to keep them from spending the nights on the buildings where their twitterings disturb people's peace and their droppings befoul the windowsills, ledges and walls of buildings. Both in Europe and in North America people have tried trapping the starlings, netting them, poisoning them, shooting them and trying to frighten them away with flares, smoke, fire hoses and a variety of noises. Among the noises used have been recordings of the alarm notes of starlings broadcast to the roosting birds in the hope that they would all take wing and fly away. Another was to use ultrasonic sounds which are known to upset some animals. In one city in central England when the ultrasonics were used some years ago the only result that anyone could see was that all the dogs in the city became restless. The starlings were quite unmoved.

Sticky pastes have been invented to paint on windowsills and ledges in the hope that the starlings would object to getting their feet dirty. This works for a time but the starlings are soon back. There seemed nothing for it but to design new buildings without ledges or sills of any kind and in some places this is being done. It must be the first time that a bird had made man change his building designs.

We often hear of animal species that are dying out or have become extinct. It is quite a change to be able to talk about one which seems to be enjoying what is almost a flush of youth, vigorous and robust and pushing out in all directions.

Using your Chest as a Dining Table

The common otters of our rivers and lakes sometimes go down to the sea to feed and some of them spend most of their time on the shore, going into the sea to hunt. Because of this people sometimes speak of river otters and sea otters. This is all right until we remember that there is another animal that has been called the sea otter. It lives in the North Pacific, all along the coast from California up to Alaska, then along the Aleutian Islands and off the coast of Asia as far south as Kamchatka. The sea otter very seldom comes on land. It spends all its time floating on its back among the kelp beds, the masses of large floating seaweeds just off shore. It feeds on clams, sea urchins and crabs and to get these it dives to the bottom of the sea, sometimes as deep as 120 feet.

Centuries ago the sea otter was very plentiful all round these North Pacific coasts. It has a very valuable fur and some of the North American Indians, those redskins living near the coast, used to catch a few sea otters to use their fur. They caught so few compared with the large numbers of sea otters there were that it made very little difference to their total numbers. Then Europeans started to explore North America and they discovered the sea otter. They also discovered what a beautiful fur it had, so they started to kill the animals and send their skins back to the London markets. The people living in Asia, along the Pacific coast had also begun hunting the sea otter. In fact they were so zealous in their search for more and more sea otter skins that eventually they came to Alaska. These people were Russians and that is why Alaska was once owned by Russia.

By the early years of this century the numbers of sea otters had dwindled badly, so much so that in places like the coast of California the sea otter was thought to have

The sea otter is one of the few animal tool users, here it cracks a crab on a stone.

been completely wiped out. By this time the numbers of these animals remaining were so low that it was almost not worthwhile trying to hunt them. This is the danger point for any species, for although it means that men no longer go out to kill them it does mean that should any natural catastrophe overtake them, even a minor one, the species may very well become totally extinct. In this case a particularly severe winter might have wiped out the few remaining sea otters, whereas if there had been large numbers of them some would be bound to survive. That is the ever present fear, in these days of conservation, not so much that man may wipe out a species but that he may reduce its numbers to such a low point that a minor natural adversity may endanger the whole of the tiny population.

Happily the danger to the sea otter was realized in time and the United States government with the governments of Canada and Russia enacted laws to protect it. So the sea otter is no longer threatened although it is only slowly building up its numbers and going back to live among kelp beds where it had previously been killed off.

It was soon after the sea otter began to return to the coast of California that an American woman scientist, Edna Fisher, was watching sea otters and made an interesting discovery. She noticed that when a sea otter came to the surface after having dived to the sea bottom, it brought up a large flat stone as well as a clam, sea urchin or crab. It would then turn on its back, place the stone on its chest, hold the crab or clam in both paws high up over the stone, then crash it down. The sea otter would do this until the shell was broken and the otter could feed on the flesh. The operation was not as easy as it sounds because the otter would have to hammer 40 to 50 times on the stone before cracking the shell of its prey.

Miss Fisher was not able to photograph the sea otter doing this but she made several drawings of it, and she wrote a description of what she had seen. These she published in a scientific journal. Fellow zoologists, when they read what she had written and saw her drawings, were too polite to say that they did not believe her, but they did raise their eyebrows in some surprise. The reason for this is that the front paws of the sea otter have very short toes so that each paw looks little better than a stump. It seemed to these scientists that no animal with paws like that could grasp anything, let alone bring up from the sea bottom not only the crab or clam that it was going to eat but also a stone anvil on which it was going to smash it.

Many people have studied the sea otter since then and there have been photographs and films taken of it which show beyond any doubt that Edna Fisher had given the world no more than the exact truth about what the sea otter did. Those studying this animal since then have found that it can do something more remarkable. Having eaten one clam or crab, as the case may be, it will then dive to the bottom of the sea to get another one. It actually takes its stone with it and it comes to the surface again with the same stone to be used as an anvil for its second victim. It does this not by grasping the stone but by holding it in its armpit. Indeed, whenever it is not used, the stone is tucked under its armpit in case it is needed again shortly. We can be in no doubt about this either because scientists have filmed sea otters doing this. They are able to see with their binoculars, while the sea otter is at work, or can see from their films, the shape and the markings of the flat stone which show clearly that it is the identical stone being carried to the seabed and brought up again.

All this is fascinating. It is especially interesting because very few animals are known to use a tool. That was another reason why the scientists raised their eyebrows at first. Now comes the moral to this story. Had the sea otter become extinct before Edna Fisher watched it we should never have known that this remarkable animal was capable of using a tool with its stumpy paws. Had anybody noticed it before the days of cameras and had merely written it in a book, nobody would have believed it. Had the sea otter not been saved from extinction until the time when cameras had reached their high efficiency, there would have been nothing to back up such a story and to give the much needed proof.

A Strong and Unpleasant Smell

The hoatzin is an unusual bird from the moment it is hatched. It lives in the shrubby trees growing along the banks of the rivers of the Amazon basin, in South America. Two or three white eggs, with brown spots, are laid on a platform of sticks between 5 and 20 feet up from the ground. From each of these hatches a chick which is almost naked and looks like some queer reptile. On each wing it has two strong claws and soon after hatching the chick starts to creep about the nest, on all fours. Before long it is crawling from the nest and clinging to the branches of the trees.

It sometimes happens that the chick falls into the river. That does not bother it. It simply swims to the bank, using its legs and its wings, clambers up the bank and then climbs up the tree, back to the nest. In climbing it uses its feet as well as the claws on its wings, and it also uses its strong beak, parrot-fashion. Not only do they fall in the water accidentally, chicks have been seen to jump into the water to escape capture.

When it is two to three weeks old the baby hoatzin grows its feathers and at the same time loses the claws on its wings. In time it grows into a bird that looks like a somewhat odd pheasant. It is brownish with white flecks on the neck, back and wings. It has strong legs, a long slender neck, very small head and a loose top-knot of feathers. The skin on the sides of its face is bright blue and its eyes are red. And it has eyelashes.

Although it is two feet long the hoatzin weighs only 28 ounces, little more than a wood pigeon, which is much smaller. This is because so much of it is tail feathers and wings and also it has such a large crop. The front part of the gullet of other birds is swollen to form a bag in which food is stored

when it is first swallowed. The hoatzin feeds on the leaves, buds, flowers and fruit of only three or four kinds of shrub or tree. These are not easy to digest and the bird must eat a lot of them to get enough nourishment. So not only is its crop double but it takes up a third of the inside of the body. It has to be large to store a lot of leaves and it is also muscular because it acts as a gizzard to grind the food to pieces to digest it. This unusually large crop throws the rest of the bird out of balance.

Anyone who has seen a chicken being carved for the table knows that it has a large breastbone with a high ridge or keel on it. The keel is needed to hold the large muscles used for flapping the wings when the bird flies. Indeed, the breast of chicken, as we call it, which supplies most of the meat, is made up of these large flight muscles. Because the hoatzin has such a large crop the breastbone has been pushed out of its usual place. The front half of it bends up at right angles so that it does not interfere with the crop. Moreover, the keel is only small so the flight muscles are small. As a result the hoatzin cannot fly well. It can do little more than spread its wings and glide down from the trees. It will then climb back using its feet and heave itself over the branches with its wings. It will also flap its wings to keep its balance when perched on a branch, for although its legs and toes look strong the bird cannot perch securely.

Other birds that perch can grip a branch so firmly with their toes that even a high wind will not dislodge them. The hoatzin cannot do this. It holds on with its toes but leans forward so that it is resting on the rear half of its breastbone. As a result the breast there is covered with a hard skin. Indeed, it uses its breast like a third leg. Or perhaps we should say it is the main leg because the true legs, being weak, do little more than help balance the bird as it rests on its breast on the branch.

The curious name of this bird is said to be in imitation of its harsh screech. Although the hoatzin is rare and is found only in patches along the river banks there is little danger of its becoming extinct. It is not easy to find in the waterside forest and nobody wants to eat it because it has such a strong and unpleasant smell. It has many other names, two of them being the stink bird and the stinking pheasant.

Natural History Quiz

1. Some of the collective names of animals are amusing. Familiar examples are: a gaggle of geese, a murmuration of starlings, a charm of goldfinches and a pride of lions. What do we call a flock of peacocks?

2. What is a mandrake, plant or animal?

3. Are elephants afraid of mice?

4. What is a pit viper?

5. What is the Resurrection plant?

6. Can you tell the difference between a pigeon and a dove?

7. What do we mean when we say someone is shrewd? Does it have anything to do with the animal we call a shrew?

S C Bisserot / Bruce Coleman Ltd

Answers on Page 78

How Animals Forecast the Weather

At the age of three I was staying with my grandmother in September. Even today I clearly remember her saying to a robin that had landed near the house: 'Go away you rascal.' Only when I had grown up did I understand why this was said. A robin coming near the house in autumn is said to foretell an early or a severe winter. Another old belief, which also goes back centuries, is that a robin coming into the house means frost or snow.

Robin redbreast has long been looked upon as a weather prophet:

> If the robin sings in the bush,
> Then the weather will be coarse;
> If the robin sings on the barn,
> Then the weather will be warm.

Many people will tell you that when a cat washes behind its ears or when it rushes about the house restlessly it is a sign of rain. The second of these is almost certainly correct. You will often hear people say that it is going to rain because the cows are lying down, but since cows lie down from time to time throughout every day this is hardly a good guide. On the other hand, when swallows are flying high people say it is a sign of good weather to come. There is more truth in this because swallows and also martins and swifts feed on flying insects and these tend to go higher in good weather.

Many people, and especially those who study the weather, are apt to pooh-pooh these sayings and beliefs, calling them old wives' tales. They take the view that animals will tell you what the weather is like when it has arrived but do not tell you in advance. Rather like the Devon farmer, who told my daughter: 'When you see dragonflies flying it isn't raining.'

I am not sure that this is always true.

Jane Burton

The cheeky robin redbreast is said to signal a hard winter when it stays near to a house during the Autumn.

Last year, for example, a flower festival was being held in our village church and one of the ladies responsible for the decorations looked up at the sky and said: 'I hope it doesn't rain. It is such a nuisance when one is carrying flowers about.' The person to whom she said this replied: 'The shepherdess says it is not going to rain.'

The barometer was low that day, the weather forecast as given in the News Bulletin was for rain. The sky looked overcast and every other sign seemed to portend rain. Throughout the day, about every hour or so, we had just a few spots of rain and no more. In fact, the amount of rain was so little that had I not heard about all this in the morning I probably would not have noticed even the few spots. But it did not rain, which was what the meteorologists had told us to expect.

Two days later I happened to meet the shepherdess and I asked her why she had been so positive, because her prophecy had certainly been correct in spite of everything.

She told me you can always tell by the sheep. When the weather is fine they move onto the high ground and graze contentedly. If they move about restlessly it is going to rain. Certainly in this case the sheep were not forecasting weather that had arrived, they were giving us a correct sign of what the weather was going to be like during the next 12 hours, which is nearly as good as the Meteorological Office can do.

Some years ago, on the day of our annual fruit and vegetable show, I noticed all the swifts streaming away to the south from our village, just after the show started. Ten minutes later black clouds gathered over the valley and a violent thunderstorm burst on us, driving everybody into the marquee. When the storm was over the swifts came back. Swifts are known as rain swallows or thunder swallows. They live by hunting insects on the wing and when it is raining heavily this is impossible. At nesting time more especially the swifts must hunt incessantly if they are to feed themselves and their chicks. What they do therefore is to fly out of the path of the storm and their chicks meanwhile go into a deep sleep like that of hibernation. This has long been known in Finland where scientists have found that the swifts will suddenly fly hundreds of miles to the south and soon after they have gone the thunderstorms arrive. It is very clear that the swifts are able to detect these storms while they are still a long way off.

There is a fish that lives in the muddy rivers of Europe which is known as the weatherfish. It is a loach yellow to grey in colour and up to a foot long. This loach grows very restless, so we are told, 24 hours

Jane Burton / Bruce Coleman Ltd

Dragonflies rarely fly on rainy days but if the weather is fine and settled their dancing flight is a common sight.

before there is a thunderstorm. Scientists differ in their opinions about this. Some do not believe it, others say that the fish seems sensitive to changes in the barometric pressure. Unfortunately no experiments have been made to test this. Nevertheless, the general belief of people living in districts where the loaches live is very firm that this is a weatherfish.

How can a fish forecast weather? Does it have special senses or how does it do it? We do not know the answer to these questions but there is a belief, and a very ancient one, that sharks know when storms are building up and in Bermuda a very old method of forecasting weather is to have a flask half filled with shark oil. That is, the oil from a shark's body. This oil changes as the conditions in the atmosphere change by becoming cloudy or clear. The local people swear by this as a way of forecasting the weather. They even say that the oil changes with the tides every six hours and with the phases of the moon. They point out that weather always comes with the moon and goes with the tides, because the tides and the moon work together.

There may or may not be any truth in this but at least it suggests how the weatherfish and other animals may be able to detect the weather to come, by slight changes going on inside their bodies as simple as the change in the shark's oil from clear to cloudy.

Jane Burton

Well before bad weather arrives sheep leave the hilltops and head for shelter.

Some Fishes Have Four Eyes

There are two fishes called the four-eyed fish. One about six inches long, lives in the rivers of Central and South America. The other, three times this length, lives in the seas of the north-eastern Pacific, in what is called the twilight zone.

In the freshwater four-eyed fish, there is one eye on each side set high up on the head and it is divided into two halves by a dark horizontal band. The fish swims just under the surface so that the level of the water is exactly along the dark band. The upper half of the eye is above water level and watches for insects on the surface of the water, the lower half watches for insects swimming just under the surface.

The marine four-eyed fish is altogether different. The twilight zone in the sea is between 300 and 3,000 feet down. During the day only a small amount of light reaches these depths, giving just a blue glimmer. Most fishes living there have large eyes and even then are only able to see things that are nearby. So they have to wait for their food to come to them. They do not need to swim fast.

Nobody has been down to see how the four-eyed fish lives but the shape of its body tells its own story. The body is long, narrow and torpedo-shaped. In front is a large mouth. The fins are set well back on the body. In fact, the four-eyed fish is shaped like a pike. We know a pike lies in wait for

its victim and then makes a quick dart at it. Only a fish shaped like this and with the fins set well back can go in for these sudden lightning-like rushes.

If a fish catches its food in this way then we know it must be able to keep watch all round itself and it must have eyes that help it to judge distances well. Otherwise it would miss its target. And that is exactly what we find in this particular fish. Each of its eyes is large and the pupil looks upwards and outwards. The retina in each is made up of millions of cells known as rods. The retina in our eyes is made up of two kinds of cells, rods and cones. The rods are slender cells and work best in dim light. The cones work best in bright light. So the eyes of the marine four-eyed fish see well in the dim blue light.

At the lower edge of each of the large eyes is a small eye, almost like a bud on the large eye. This is highly sensitive, for judging distances. There are also two swellings above the small eye, like extra lenses. They do not have a retina and they probably bend light rays onto the lens of the large eye so that it can see what is behind and perhaps below it.

So altogether the marine four-eyed fish has two large eyes for good all-round vision and also two small eyes for focussing on a target. This, however, is almost certainly not the whole story because, from the few specimens brought up from the depths of the twilight zone, we know the small eyes can be swivelled around independently of the large eye, perhaps to scan a wider area.

A freshwater four-eyed fish has divided eyes to look for food above and below the surface.

Tiny Beetles Kill Elm Trees

The English elm is a tall tree and it throws out suckers so that wherever there is a well-grown elm we see smaller ones growing up around it. Elms are usually in rows for where a tree has been growing in a hedge all the suckers get cut down or trampled down except those that are growing in the hedge in line with the parent tree.

Elms whether single or in rows are a common feature of the English countryside.

Elm trees that are stricken with Dutch elm disease stand out from healthy specimens as the leaves become discoloured and instead of being a rich green they are pale and yellowish.

Indeed, they are so common that we almost forget they are there—until something happens to them. In 1971 the newspapers were filled with the warning that we might lose all our elms and that this would make a great change to our English countryside. The reason for this was that the elms were struck by a disease known as the Dutch elm disease.

In a way, this is a fairly new disease in trees. It is believed to have come from Asia, although nobody quite knows from where or when it came, or even how. It was first noticed in France in 1918 but did not do a great deal of damage. Six years later it reached Holland and there it did tremendous damage, which is why it is called the Dutch elm disease. A few years later there was a serious outbreak of the disease in North America because timber had been imported from Europe.

All this time the disease had been in Britain but did not attract attention because very few elms had caught it, or if they had they had not died of it. We do not know the full truth about this disease yet but it is believed that every now and then a more virulent strain of it appears causing these widespread outbreaks in the trees in a particular country.

The disease is due to a fungus which attacks the tree, rots its wood and causes the leaves to go yellow. It is usually a change in the colour of the leaves that acts as a warning signal that the trees are diseased. The real culprit, however, is a very small beetle, one of a family known as bark beetles or engraver beetles. These burrow under the bark of a tree and lay their eggs. If they carry the spores of the fungus on

The bark beetle that causes all the trouble is only a quarter of an inch long.

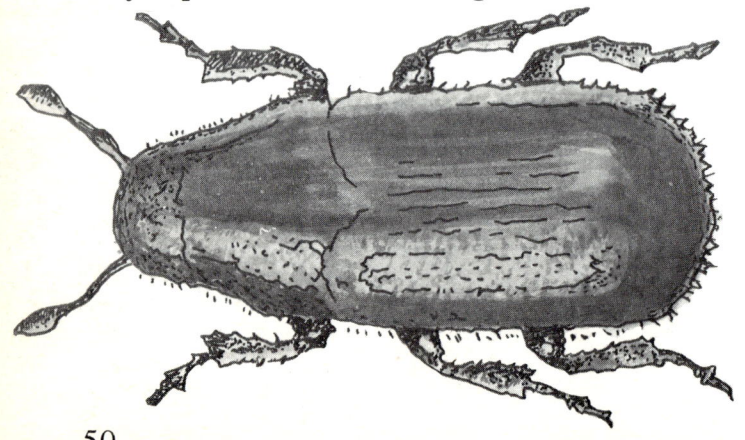

their bodies when they bore into the bark then that tree becomes diseased.

Bark beetles are usually only about $\frac{1}{4}$ inch long, often less. A pair of them about to mate bore through the bark to the wood. Then they start to bore a horizontal tunnel and the female lays her eggs at intervals along it. The eggs hatch and the larvae from them tunnel at right angles to this main tunnel, feeding on the wood. As each larva grows larger so its tunnel gets slightly wider and there comes a time when it turns into a pupa at the end of the tunnel. After a while each pupa turns into an adult beetle which eats its way out again through the bark. So the bark becomes punctured by many holes that let in moisture and the spores of fungi. Besides being attacked by the fungus the beetle has brought in, the bore holes may let in the wet causing further damage to the tree. The spores of other fungi can also come in through these bore holes.

You can often see the borings of bark beetles and engraver beetles on a dead tree by pulling away the bark. Then you can see the beautiful designs made by their tunnels both on the inside of the bark and on the surface of the wood exposed when the bark is pulled off. It is a pity to think that such beautiful designs can be so damaging to sturdy trees. It probably would not be so bad for the trees but for the numbers of beetles that infest them. Some years ago a German scientist made a count of the number of beetles infesting a single large oak tree and he gave us the figure of 80,000 beetles. This seems incredible, until you come to look into it. A little while ago I sawed off a dead branch from a beech tree. It was about six feet long and two inches in diameter, really quite a small branch. I counted 103 separate patterns made by bark beetles' families. Since each of these patterns was made by a pair of beetles and their larvae, and as each pair had produced at least 20 larvae, we can say that this small branch was infested by something like 2,000 beetles at least. Even if the count made by the German scientist meant 80,000 adult bark beetles, or 40,000 pairs, infesting a single tree, and ignored their offspring, it would still be possible to believe it.

Goliath and Methuselah Trees

Opposite my study window are two cedars of Lebanon, planted in 1650. The last time they were measured they were 103 feet high. A tall man is six feet high so these cedars are as high as 20 tall men standing on each other's shoulders. Even this does not help us much in trying to form an idea of height in trees.

When I first came to live here, many dead branches had fallen from the tops of these cedars and had become lodged high up in the tree. Had one of these fallen in a high wind onto somebody passing underneath it might have hurt that person. So to avoid this danger I paid four men to go up into the trees to dislodge the branches, which then fell to the ground and could be taken away and burnt.

I was interested in the way the men, without ladders, swarmed up the trees. But when one of them had reached nearly to the top and he stood balancing on the branch without holding, I became dizzy and went indoors so that I could not see him. I am a coward about heights. Certainly for me, merely watching, 103 feet is a dizzy height.

Would these men have climbed so willingly the tallest trees in the world? A eucalyptus tree in Australia is said to be the tallest at 450 feet—or 90 tall men standing on each other's shoulders. This makes the Big tree of California look a dwarf. The tallest of these, in the Sequoia National Park, is 272 feet tall and measures 75 feet round the trunk near its base. It is estimated to hold 50,000 cubic feet of timber and to weigh 1,500 tons.

Magnificent giant Karri trees grow in Western Australia. Sometimes over 200 feet high they tower over the man and car.

Australian News and Information Bureau

Although so large the Big trees were not discovered until 1841. Twelve years later seeds from them were brought to Europe. Many were planted in gardens in England and they were given the name of wellingtonia, after the Duke of Wellington, who had died just before the trees were discovered.

Another tree, the Californian redwood, also preserved in the National Park, is halfway between the eucalyptus and the Big tree for height, measuring up to 368 feet.

The most remarkable tree in the world is found in the Kalahari, near the coast, in the vicinity of Walvis Bay. Its trunk is only a few inches high. It is related to pines and firs and is named Welwitschia, after Welwitsch, the German botanist, who discovered it. Somebody once said that if you pulled it out of the ground it would look like an enormous carrot. The top of this wooden 'carrot' is 18 inches out of the

The Welwitschia is found in the dry Kalahari Desert of south west Africa.

ground but it is more than three feet across and it has only two leaves. These are like long ribbons about ten feet long and two feet across, and they are usually split into narrow strips for much of their length. The leaves lie straggling over the sand either side of the main trunk—the 18-inch top of the 'carrot'.

Then come the natural questions: how old are these trees and what is the oldest tree in the world? We can count the rings on the stump when a tree has been felled but it is not so easy to tell the age of a tree, and especially of a really old tree, while it is still standing. So the ages of trees are apt to be exaggerated. It seems possible, however, that the Big Tree of Tule, in Mexico, which

is a bald cypress, is between 6,000 and 7,000 years old. If true, this was already well grown when the pharaohs ruled in Ancient Egypt. Although not a giant in height, compared with the redwoods and Californian Big trees, the Big Tree of Tule has a tremendously thick trunk, 105 feet in circumference. Another long-lived tree was the Great Dragon's-blood tree, of Teneriffe, which was blown down in 1869. It was said to be 6,000 years old.

The more one reads about the ages of trees the harder it is to believe anything one reads or anything one hears about it. One of the first difficulties is that when a tree is very old it is likely to start rotting at the centre. When it is felled, all one can do is to count the rings in the sound wood and try to estimate how many annual rings there may have been in the part that is rotted.

The one tree about which there seems to be the most uncertainty and the most exaggeration is the yew. The Fortingall yew in Perthshire, Scotland, is said by some people to be 3,000 years old, but it is doubtful whether any living yew is much more than 1,000 years old and most are much less than this.

What happens is that when a yew dies the large trunk, hollow at the centre, remains for a very long time. There was such a trunk near my house. It was more than three feet in diameter, about seven feet high and no more than a shell. A man could stand inside it comfortably. There was no bark on

Showing its age a little, this very old Japonica tree is one of five trees imported into Britain from China in 1753.

This baobab tree is reputed to be 1,000 years old. The huge bottle-like trunk stores water to help it survive drought.

it and the surface was completely weather-worn. It had been like that as long as any-body living could remember. At a guess, the tree may have died centuries ago. The one thing we know is that yew wood becomes almost as hard as iron when dead and seems never to rot.

A few years ago this ancient shell of yew had to be removed. The woodman whose job it was decided that the easier way to get rid of it would be to light a fire inside it. It took a week to burn.

No doubt the tree was a thousand years old when it died. Then, as the centuries passed, and the dead trunk still continued to stand there, people added these to its real age. Possibly this particular yew was a seedling when the Romans invaded Britain nearly 2,000 years ago. So it had been there all that time but in stating its age people would forget that it may have been dead for up to a thousand years.

In the early years of the 19th century a Swiss botanist, named De Candolle, studied the ages of trees. He gave as maximum ages 4,000 to 6,000 years for the yew, 1,500 for the oak, 1,100 for the lime, 750 for the plane and 570 for the larch. This set a fashion for exaggerating the ages of trees. There is no proof of a yew living more than 1,000 years or an oak living more than 750 years. The other three probably do not reach anything like this number of years.

To show how easily mistakes are made we can turn to a cedar of Lebanon in Thames

The Australian gum or eucalyptus trees are some of the biggest in the world and some species measure over 400 feet high.

Ditton near London. King John was said to have sat under it, which would make it over 700 years old. But the cedar of Lebanon was first brought to Britain in the early part of the 17th century. So the Thames Ditton cedar could not be much more than 300 years old. The famous catalpa tree in Gray's Inn, London, was said to have been planted by Francis Bacon. The catalpa is a native of North America. Bacon died in 1626. The catalpa was not introduced into Britain until 1726.

We can measure the height of a tree accurately. We can tell the age of a healthy tree by counting the rings. But there will probably always be uncertainty about the ages of long-lived trees.

53

The Narwhal's Ten Foot Tusk

Everybody has heard of the narwhal and most of us have a fair idea what it looks like. Very few of us have seen it alive or are likely to do so. It is a whale, but not a very big one, at most about 16 feet long. But it is remarkable for the long spiral tusk that sticks out from the front of its head. This may be nearly as long as the whale itself.

We are unlikely to see narwhals because they live in the north polar seas, high up in the Arctic in the waters around the North Pole, although a single narwhal has sometimes come as far south as the British Isles. This is, however, a very rare event. It is not that narwhals are themselves scarce. They usually go about in what are called pods, of anything from 5 to 50. Sometimes as many as two or three thousand will be seen all together in one pod and some people claim to have seen as many as 10,000.

The name 'narwhal' means 'whale corpse'. This is because of its colour. The young narwhal is bluish-grey all over but as it grows this colour becomes lighter especially on the sides and the belly. When fully grown it is greyish-white with dark grey or black spots on the back. Whether this greyish-white suggests the 'pallor of death' or not we have to leave to those who have actually seen a narwhal alive. To us who are ignorant of the animal it seems a poor reason for calling it 'whale corpse'. Perhaps there is some other reason for the name which has been lost in the mists of time.

For nearly a thousand years, at least, the narwhal has been known to the people of Europe and Asia because of its valuable tusk. Only the male narwhal has this tusk which is a long canine tooth growing out from the left side of the skull. There is a second canine tooth on the right but this seldom grows out as a tusk although it can be seen in the skull when the animal is dead.

Very rarely, the second canine, the right-hand one, will also grow out as a tusk so that a very few males have been known to have two tusks instead of the usual one. Usually the female narwhal shows no tusks although she has the two canine teeth in her skull; exceptionally one may grow out as it does in the head of the male. The tusk itself is spirally twisted and it always has a right-hand spiral whether there is one tusk or two.

The reason why the narwhal became so well known was that its tusk was sent back from the Arctic by the early Viking explorers and was believed to be the horn of the unicorn. Indeed, the narwhal was also known as the sea unicorn. Narwhal tusk was believed to have unusual virtues, the most noted of which was that it would show whether food was poisoned or not. In those days of long ago when nobody could trust his neighbour and killing a rival by poisoning his food was a common practice, anything that helped in this way was almost beyond price. So narwhal tusk was worth its weight in gold. Anyone afraid of being poisoned would place the narwhal tusk on the table where food was being set for him and he would watch it to see whether it would turn colour. In addition to this there was the belief that if a man had actually taken poison the best antidote was to swallow powdered narwhal tusk.

One of the first people to write about the narwhal was Martin Frobisher who lived in the 16th century and was a sailor and explorer. He it was who set out in a 25-ton ship to look for the northwest passage to the East. When he found land he thought he had reached Asia but he was in fact at Greenland. He tells in his account of the voyage of an experiment made with a narwhal tusk.

Those who wanted a piece of the tusk for detecting poison merely cut off the tip, this small piece being enough for their purpose. When this is done it can be seen that there is a hollow running through the tusk. Martin Frobisher told how his sailors put spiders into the hollow centre of the tusk after the tip had been broken off and he reports that the spiders very soon died. This was sufficient proof, for the men of that time, that narwhal tusk was an antidote to poison. Anything that could kill a spider so quickly must be a powerful charm against the evil of poisoning, they thought. Unfortunately for the experiment, Frobisher confessed in his writing that he had not seen the experiment himself but that he believed it because it was 'reported unto him of a truth'.

The Esquimaux have long valued the narwhal but in a different way. They hunt it for food. A well-grown narwhal means a ton or two of meat and blubber and the skin is particularly valuable because it is very rich in vitamin C. The Esquimaux call it muktuk and they eat it raw. It chews like rubber and tastes like hazel nuts.

Because narwhals live high up in the Arctic, out at sea well away from land, we know very little about how they live, except that they feed mainly on cuttlefish although they will sometimes eat fish as well. The biggest puzzle about the narwhal is, however, what does the male do with its tusk? Some people have said that it uses it to poke holes through the ice so that it can breathe. Others claim that male narwhals fight each other with their tusks, using them as rapiers. The third view is that the tusk is used to stir up the seabed when the narwhal is looking for food. Clearly, these must be wrong because the obvious question to ask is how does the female get on without any tusk to help with her breathing or her search for food or as a weapon of defence? The only thing we can suppose is that the narwhal tusk is like the antlers of a stag, a male adornment that has very little use apart from impressing a female.

Narwhals have mottled grey and white bodies which become whiter with age. Their most distinctive feature is the male's long spiral-threaded tusk which is actually a very elongated canine tooth. Sometimes this grows up to ten feet long and seven inches round.

Field Mouse Treasure Hoarders

One day I returned home to find a neighbour had left a note in my letter box asking me to call on him. This I did and he took me into his garden and showed me a little pile of pebbles in one of his flowerbeds. It was just over 2 inches across at its base and there was a small arched entrance on one side. Looking through this we could see the opening to the burrow of a field mouse, the one known as the long-tailed field mouse or wood mouse. It looked like a miniature of those piles of rock that men make, known as cairns. This is the name I have used ever since I saw this first one, although from the way it was built it could just as easily have been called an igloo. I could see no sign on the earth around the cairn of footprints that would tell me what had built it. We could only suspect that it was a field mouse, so I dusted the earth around with a white powder in the hope that when I went back the next day I should find the tracks of whatever was living there. This also failed, so I set a trap to catch the unknown animal alive, and in the next few days caught six field mice.

One of these I took home and put it in a vivarium, hoping I had found the master builder and that it would repeat its performance. The vivarium was a glass tank $2\frac{1}{2} \times 1 \times 1$ foot and in this I placed earth and a number of small pebbles and some food for the

Below. A field mouse hoards hazelnuts for the winter in a little underground nut store.

A long-tailed field mouse climbs a sticky bud, using its tail to help it balance. ▶

mouse. Over the top of the vivarium I placed two sheets of glass which met in the middle, giving a chink of space to let in the air. The mouse ate some food. It also made a burrow, but the following day it had managed somehow to push the sheets of glass aside and escape.

I took home some of the others I caught later and put them in a vivarium but none of them built a cairn.

Each of the mice weighed about $\frac{3}{4}$ ounce and the largest of the pebbles used in making the cairn weighed $\frac{1}{3}$ ounce, and since these would have had to be gathered and transported from various points on the flowerbed, the building of the cairn must have meant a fair amount of labour. So presumably the mice building it were not doing it for the fun of it. But if not, then the question remained, what was the use of it?

I asked several naturalist friends whether they had ever seen this. All except one said they had not. That one person said: 'They often do this.' I was a little surprised to hear him say this because I had not found anything about it in any book on natural history that I had looked at. Moreover, it is 17 years since I saw this first one and I have only found one other in all that time although I have examined many mouse burrows. Indeed I must have looked at hundreds of them, looking specially for some sign of a cairn.

So there were two questions that had to be answered. The first was, how often do mice do this? The other was, why do they do it? And both questions still remain unanswered, although I know a little more about the subject.

For example, a few years ago, somebody wrote to me saying that he had found a little pile of stones beside a mouse hole in his lawn. Since he was about to mow the lawn he picked up this pile of pebbles and threw them aside on a flowerbed, so as not to damage the blade of his mower. He mowed the lawn, and the following day he noticed that all the little pebbles had been picked up from where he threw them and put together in a pile beside the same mouse hole. This was interesting but did not get me any further.

Shortly after this my gardener told me of a little pile of pebbles beside a mouse hole under the leaves of a cucumber plant in one of the cold frames. It was not igloo-shaped, like the first one I saw, but merely a pile of little pebbles beside the hole. So far as I could see it could have no value for the mice unless it marked the spot where the entrance to the burrow was, so enabling the mice to dive quickly into it if they were in danger. After all men make cairns to mark a spot they especially wish to remember, such as the grave of an explorer, or a place where some important event took place. Could it be that the mouse was marking the entrance to the burrow deliberately? If so, why do not more of them mark the entrance in this way?

About this time I happened to catch a field mouse and again put it in a vivarium with a lot of earth but no pebbles. The strange thing is that it built a cairn after it had made a burrow in the earth and it made the cairn of small round pellets of earth each about one eighth of an inch diameter. This began to make it look as though some field mice just cannot help piling pebbles, or other things, near their mouse hole. And this was borne out by somebody who wrote to me that he had found a pile of lead shot beside a field mouse burrow.

The only thing I have to add is that a lady wrote to me saying that she had been watching a field mouse that had babies coming in and out of its burrow and when she came to examine it she found there was a pile of stones just inside the burrow. She suggested that perhaps it was a way the mother mouse had of stopping her babies from wandering out of the nest before it was time for them to do so. So here was another theory, and the only other one that has been put forward was about the first cairn I saw, when my neighbour who showed it to me suggested that the mice might have built it to keep the rain out of the burrow. I believe none of these theories holds water. I would be more inclined to think that it is something to do with the habit we find in so many mice and rats of hoarding food.

The long-tailed field mouse is very much given to hoarding food. You sometimes find buried in the garden about a pint of hazel nuts or walnuts, and people then suppose that a squirrel has buried them there. In spite of the popular idea that squirrels do this, neither the red squirrel nor the grey squirrel that live in Britain bury nuts in this way. They bury them one at a time well spaced out. Such hoards are the work of the long-tailed field mouse, who will bury hoards of nuts, acorns or berries. Some years ago I was digging out a compost heap in the garden and came across a hoard of holly berries. The mouse was still at work on it when I disturbed it. During the course of the day I dug out the compost and spread it over the garden, and in doing so I spread

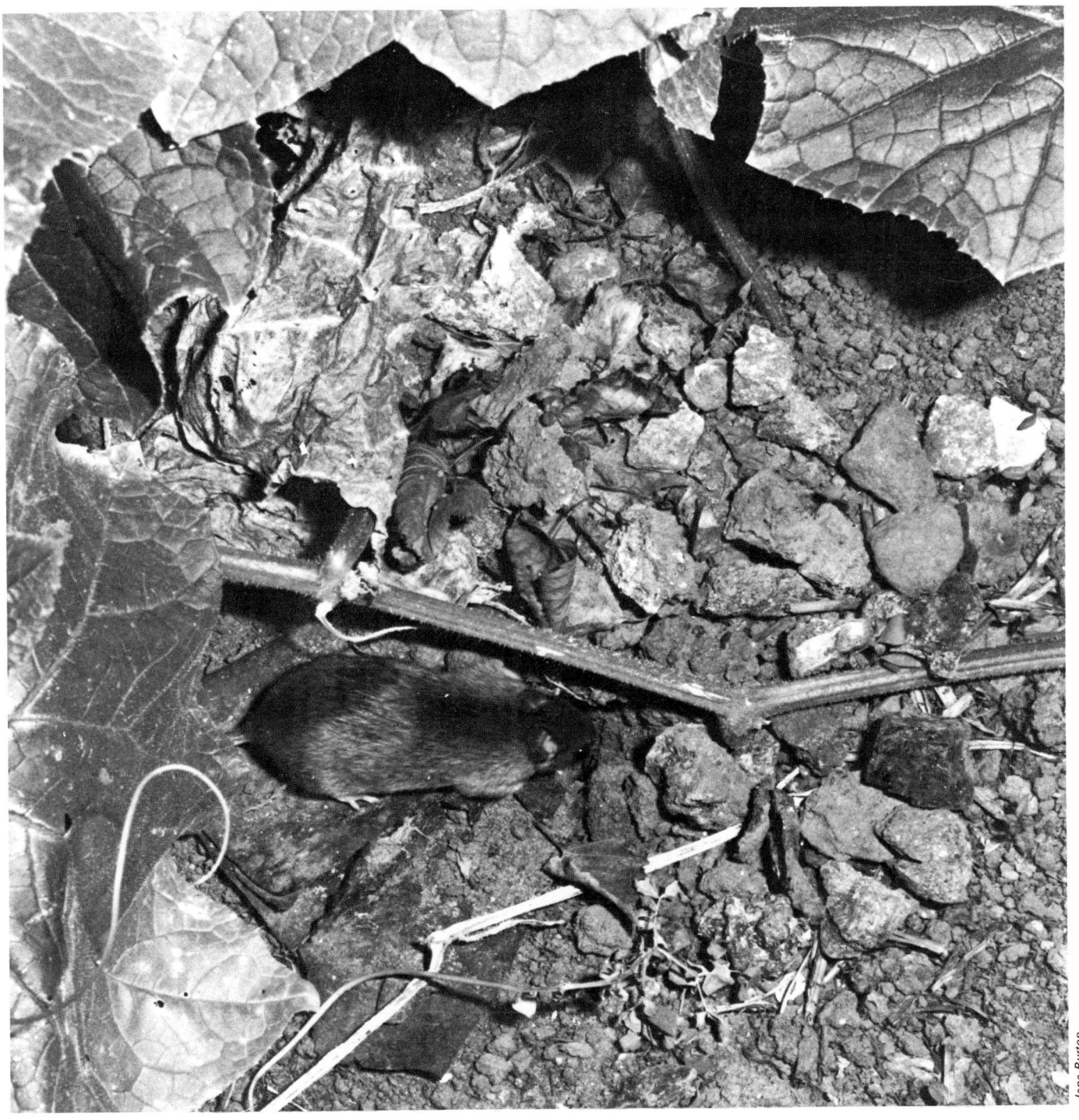

Jane Burton

A little field mouse busies itself with a building operation. It has gathered pebbles and stones to make a little circular cairn near to its mouse hole. The stones are large in relation to its body so the field mouse must have worked very hard to construct the cairn.

59

out the holly berries too. The following day all these berries had been collected up and were back in one hoard in the compost heap. This shows how fast the mouse will work and it also gives us some idea of the drive it has to do this kind of thing.

My guess is that some field mice, but not all, make these cairns as a sort of side effect of their food hoard. If this is correct then it would explain why one naturalist said they often do it. Thus, it may be more common among the mice in one district than another and that I happened to have searched places where the habit is not common while my naturalist friend happened to have seen them in another district where the habit is common.

Food hoarding can take curious forms in some rodents. The best known is the pack rat of North America. It is called the pack rat or trade rat. This is an allusion to the packman who in years gone by was a trader who carried all his wares in a pack on his back and travelled through country districts calling at houses to sell them. The pack rat does not quite do that but it does go in for a kind of barter. Like the long-tailed field mouse it collects nuts and puts them together in a hoard but it has the strange habit of always leaving something in place of the nut it takes. There is the story of a miners' camp in which there was a box of steel nuts. When the miners came to open the box to use the nuts they found that pack rats had taken them all and had left a pebble in the place of each nut they had taken so the box was filled full of pebbles. But they make this swap with anything they take, presumably on the principle that fair exchange is no robbery.

In the autumn field mice eat whatever is available, even if it is too big to hide away.

Why did the Dinosaurs Die?

In this day and age, almost as soon as children can read, they learn about the dinosaurs, the giant reptiles that were larger than elephants. They read about the Brontosaurus with its huge body, long neck and long tail and its very small head. They also learn about the huge Tyrannosaurus, the tyrant lizard, which made the earth tremble as it walked. This, of course, cannot be true. Any animal that shook the earth

Cetiosaurus, one of the largest dinosaurs.

with its footsteps would shake itself to pieces. At least, it would jar its spine so that every step would be agony.

Although we know a great deal about what the dinosaurs looked like, what they ate and how they lived, there is still one big problem we have not solved. About 70 million years ago they suddenly became extinct. And nobody can say for certain why this happened. From the study of their fossils we know that they did not slowly die out. They suddenly died out.

The time when the giant reptiles were living lasted from 135 million years ago to 70 million years ago, a span of 65 million years. During this period there were very few birds and very few mammals, the four-footed hairy animals. So the reptiles more or less had the land to themselves. That is why we call this period the Age of Reptiles.

The dinosaurs had very small brains so we can safely say they were slow-witted. One of the first explanations put forward was that the mammals, having better brains, harassed the giant reptiles, perhaps even killed them. This we now know to be wrong. The few mammals there were then were only the size of a shrew, two to three inches long.

Then the idea was put forward that the giant reptiles suddenly became extinct because the tiny shrew-like mammals ate their eggs. Had this been so, the reptiles would have died out gradually.

Some of the suggestions were that the climate changed suddenly, that it became too warm for the dinosaurs, too cold, too dry or too wet. Other scientists suggested that they had trouble with their food. Some thought they might have eaten too much, others that they did not get enough. Perhaps they did not get enough of the right kind. This last suggestion was made because of changes known to have taken place in the plants. Before the Age of Reptiles the main plants had been ferns. Then flowering plants began to replace these, so the dinosaurs may have suffered from too little fern oil.

One way in which flowering plants differ from ferns is that their stems and leaves are more tough and fibrous. Many flowering plants have glass-like silica in their stem, which could have ruined the dinosaur's teeth so that they starved. Or they may have contained poisons.

Perhaps disease broke out among the dinosaurs, or their brains grew too small so that they became more stupid than ever. They might have had too many parasites, or suffered from slipped discs in the backbone, too few hormones or too many hormones.

It may be that changes in the atmosphere caused the downfall of the dinosaurs. The flowering plants may have caused too much oxygen in the air, there may have been floods, the swamps may have dried up. There may have been shifts in the earth's poles. There may have been poisonous gases in the air or volcanic dust. Meteorites may have bombarded the Earth, or comets, or the Earth may have been thrown out of balance when the moon was shot off from what is now the Pacific Ocean.

Any of these causes would have made the dinosaurs die out gradually. What we have to find out is why they suddenly disappeared from the face of the Earth. Last year, in 1971, a Canadian and an American scientist put forward yet another idea. They suggest that their death was caused by the explosion of a supernova, a star exploding with great violence in outer space and with a brightness thousands of millions of times greater than our sun. It can best be thought of as an unimaginably super-nuclear explosion. This would send out cosmic rays and gamma rays, as well as X-rays. Their effect on the climate of the earth would be catastrophic, but would not last long. The air would suddenly grow very cold, but this would last only a week perhaps. So it would not produce an Ice Age or leave traces which scientists would be able to find millions of years later. All that would be left for scientists to examine today would be the skeletons of large numbers of animals wiped out by the cold. Some animals would survive, however, so that life would go on, but those animal species that could not stand up to the cold would be wiped out. Perhaps rubbed out would be a better way of putting it and maybe this was what really happened to the huge dinosaurs who, like present day reptiles, were very sensitive to any violent change in temperature.

Yawn: Signal to Attack

Some years ago I was standing in front of the large eel tank in the Aquarium of the London Zoo. There were several congers swimming about but one was lying in a drainpipe in the foreground of the tank. It lay there more or less without moving for quite a long time, then it yawned. It gave a huge yawn and a few minutes later swam out of the drainpipe and continued swimming round and round the tank.

I had always supposed that the conger had done what we do after we have been asleep. That is to say, we yawn as part of waking ourselves up. Only last year did we learn that somebody has been studying why fishes yawn, and what he has found changes the picture.

First of all, perhaps, we should see why it is we yawn. We do so when we are tired, before going to bed, and we do so first thing in the morning after waking. When we yawn in the evening it is because our muscles are tired and the yawn makes us fill our lungs deeply and drives the blood from the lungs to the heart. So more oxygen is carried to the heart, the heart pumps this to the muscles and this makes the muscles work better. That is, it banishes fatigue.

The effect is very much the same when we yawn on waking. While we have been asleep the flow of blood round the body has slowed down and is sluggish in our veins. We stretch and this squeezes the veins, sending the blood more quickly to the heart to be purified. At the same time we yawn and this sends more oxygen to the muscles.

Fishes yawn for a different reason. To start with they yawn much more in the middle of the day than in the evening or in the morning. The middle of the day is the time when they are most active and we shall find if we watch them that when a fish has been still or moving very slowly for some time it will yawn and then start to move quickly. This means to say that it is driving the blood more quickly round its body and so giving its muscles more energy.

A fish will sometimes yawn when it is excited, when it sees an enemy or food. The reason for this is that in situations like this there is need for rapid action and the fish by yawning tones up its muscles in order to

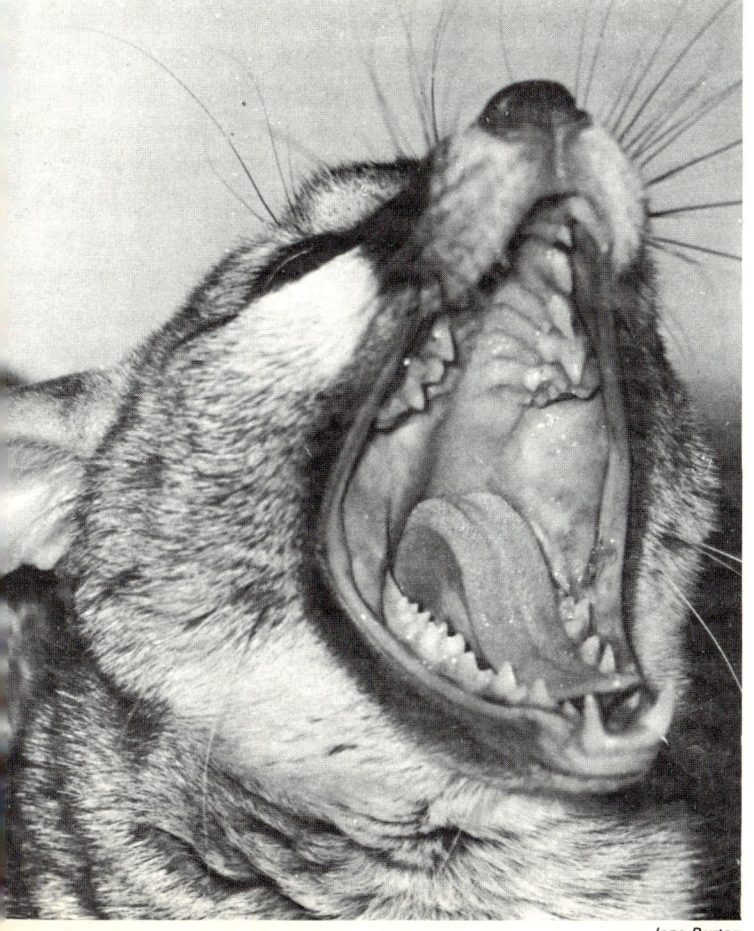

◀ A huge yawn from a Dongolan genet shows off a very fine set of teeth. The genet is related to the cat and like the domestic cat it yawns and stretches itself when it wakes up. This sends the blood moving quickly to the heart so that oxygen becomes available to give the muscles power after a day's rest.

Jane Burton

63

give it a supply of energy needed for moving quickly. There are other occasions when a fish will yawn and that is when it is thwarted. We scratch our heads or throw tantrums or do something of this sort when we are thwarted. A fish merely yawns.

There is another kind of yawning worth mentioning, and that is when a hippopotamus yawns. Most of us see this when we are visiting a zoo and we probably put it down to boredom. Often the hippopotamus will yawn when we go near the railings of its enclosure and look at it. The truth is that the hippopotamus's yawn is a signal that it is about to attack, or perhaps we should say it is the hippo's way of telling us that we are not wanted and had better go. In the wild male hippos sometimes fight over territory. It is a most awe-inspiring sight to see two of them snapping at each other with their tremendous jaws and long tusks, rearing up out of the water and lunging at each other while the water splashes high all round them as they struggle. They inflict terrible wounds on each other but surprisingly these very quickly heal, although a wounded hippo when it falls back into the water squeals with pain as the water touches the wound. These tremendous combats are always preceded by the two hippos facing each other and yawning their heads off at each other. So for a hippo a yawn is a signal that battle is about to begin.

Right . A hippopotamus yawns when it is about to attack. The huge gaping mouth issues a threat to any animal nearby and does not indicate the hippo is tired.

Peter Jackson / Bruce Coleman Ltd

Lions are thought of as very ferocious hunters. In fact they spend a great deal of time asleep in the sun and can often be seen yawning to try to wake themselves.

Below. A pike yawns as it moves slowly among the water weeds. Yawning helps to tone up its muscles so that it can put on a quick burst of speed to chase prey.

Jane Burton / Bruce Coleman Ltd

Simon Trevor / Bruce Coleman Ltd

Is the Loch Ness Monster an Otter?

Our otter is about three feet long, not quite as long as the largest domestic cat that has been measured, which was just over $3\frac{1}{2}$ feet long. Even if we take the largest of our otters ever measured, which was $5\frac{1}{2}$ feet long, it was still only medium-sized. Of the ten different kinds of otters living in the various parts of the world, the largest is the Brazilian otter and that is little more than seven feet long. So no otter can, by any stretch of the imagination, be called a monster. Yet it is possible that the lake monsters reported from all over the world may be nothing more than otters.

There is a legend about a monster in Lake Naivasha in Kenya said to have several humps and to be very long. When Theodore Roosevelt ceased to be President of the United States he went on a big game expedition to Africa. While in Kenya he was told about this monster. Roosevelt went out in a boat on the lake one day and it so hap-

Although it looks innocent enough on land an otter's body becomes sleek and sinuous in water like the curves of a monster.

Jane Burton

pened that the monster appeared, showing three humps. He shot at the middle hump. The other two disappeared, and Roosevelt found he had shot an otter. So this monster seems to have been no more than otters swimming one behind the other.

The most famous of all these lake monsters is the one supposed to be living in Loch Ness in the Scottish Highlands. For the last forty years one expedition after another has spent weeks or even months around the shores of Loch Ness in the hope of finding out what the monster could be. So far they have practically nothing to show for all their hours of watching the loch, and none of their instruments has recorded anything that can certainly be interpreted as a large unknown animal. The most favoured theory is that this monster is a plesiosaur, a large reptile that used to live in the sea but which died out 70 million years ago.

In 1971 a scientist told a meeting of the British Association for the Advancement of Science, in Cardiff, that there *is* a monster in Loch Ness. He said it was a giant wave that sometimes builds up under the surface. But this probably is only part of the story.

For some years I have been on the trail of a mystery, which has something to do with the habits of otters. Eleven years ago I read in a book, *The Spirit of the Wild*, about something an American naturalist saw in Canada, where the Canadian otter lives. He was William J. Long, at one time one of the best known naturalists in the United States. He died in 1957, at the age of 86, and for forty years he had spent his summers in the wilderness of Ontario, a large stretch of land with many large lakes that are almost unexplored.

Dr Long tells how, one evening, he saw what he thought was the sea serpent 30 to 40 feet long in one of the lakes. He almost

Otters have very flat heads which they raise out of the water in a monster-like fashion.

had to pinch himself to find out if he was dreaming. In front the serpent raised a long neck and flat snake-like head from time to time as if looking round. Then it saw Dr Long, gave out a hiss like escaping steam and disappeared beneath the water. Before then, however, Dr Long had taken a careful look with his field glasses and saw it was eight or more otters swimming in line, with the leading otter rearing up every now and then to take a look-see.

The remarkable thing is that although Dr Long had spent forty summers exploring the wilderness this was the only time he saw such a sight.

Several people have described seeing something very like this in Loch Ness and made drawings of it, but not since 1934, when the new motor road was built along the shore, and Loch Ness ceased to be a quiet, undisturbed lake.

I have tried to see otters swimming in line ever since I read Dr Long's book, but without success. I was always hoping to film them doing this. Even two otters swimming one behind the other look very like the pictures we see of the sea serpent. But I wanted to film a long line of them, six to eight, so as to have a convincing film.

Whenever I have been visiting near where there is a big lake I have not only watched for it but have asked people living there whether they have ever seen such a thing. Only once did I find a man who said he had seen it, but naturalists who have made a special study of otters not only said they had never seen it but pooh-poohed the idea.

Then I met a young American woman who said she had seen it three times, on a lake in the State of Maine, when visiting her grandmother. She made a drawing for me and it is like the drawings that used to be made at Loch Ness. She also said that now the lake had become a holiday resort. It was no longer quiet and undisturbed and she had never again seen the otters swimming in line.

Could this be the real explanation of the Loch Ness monster and other lake monsters? If so, we may never know the truth, never see a film of it. Clearly, it happens so rarely that even those studying otters have not only not seen it but disbelieve that it ever happens. Moreover, it seems that as soon as the peace of a lake is disturbed the otters give up the habit. Undisturbed lakes are becoming fewer and fewer in the world. Otters themselves are becoming less plentiful. Perhaps the chance of getting photographs or films of a procession of otters has gone for ever.

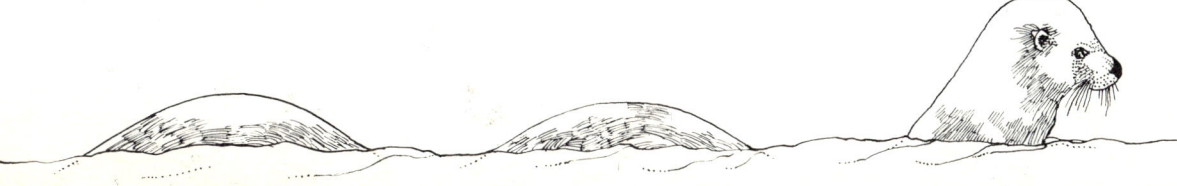

Shrews with Elephant Trunks

You might think an elephant shrew meant a very large shrew. It could be a good guess because shrews as a whole are small. The smallest of all mammals is Savi's pigmy shrew which is found in Mediterranean countries from Spain eastwards and then through southern Asia as far east as Malaya. It is also found in Africa as far south as the Cape. It is $1\frac{1}{2}$ inches long with another inch for its tail and it weighs less than an ounce. The largest land mammal is the African elephant which may weigh six tons.

By comparison with this pygmy shrew the elephant shrews are giants because the largest of them may be a foot long. That, however, is not how they get their name. It is from their long tapering snout, which looks like the beginnings of a trunk.

Even the ordinary shrews have a fairly long snout that is very flexible. A habit of these shrews is to raise the snout into the air and twitch it this way and that as if sampling the air, picking out the odours and scents borne on the wind. Whether this is really what they are doing we cannot yet say. Certainly the snout is very sensitive and it may be picking up signals other than those of smell. We are more in the dark about the snout of an elephant shrew. It is said they can wave their long snouts in circles. If so, it is even more of a puzzle what the snout is for.

Elephant shrews could just as well have been called kangaroo shrews. They have long hind legs and short front legs. They also bound along when going fast, using their hind legs for springing and the tail as a balancer, just as kangaroos do. They also use all four legs touching the ground, as a kangaroo does, when just moving about slowly. However, we do not call them kangaroo shrews but elephant shrews.

We know quite a lot about these unusual animals. We know, for example, that there are 18 different species, all African, that they live in almost every kind of country. You may find them—if you are lucky, for they give you little chance to see them—in thorn bush country, on grassy plains, in forests and thickets and in rocky country. They are often about by day but they take shelter in any crevice or crack, under logs or stones, or in other animals' burrows the moment they are alarmed. They are also given to running through tunnels in the long grass.

You are more likely to hear them. Like the true shrews they squeak in high-pitched voices. Some make a noise like a cricket. Others rap their tails on the ground and stamp rapidly with their hind feet, to give the alarm if they suspect there is danger at hand.

Another thing that is well-known is that an elephant shrew always uses the same trails if it possibly can. It soon becomes lost if it cannot do so. And the one thing we notice about these trails is that no matter how often a shrew uses a trail it always puts its feet down in the same places. Since it bounds along these at high speed we can suppose that it has either very sharp senses or a good memory, or both.

Two years ago somebody made a close study of an elephant shrew that sheds a

An elephant shrew uses its long and sensitive snout to search for termites to eat.

Above. Elephant shrews usually eat quite small insects and grubs. Here a spectacled elephant shrew is making a meal of a grasshopper which is making its cheek pouches bulge.

little light on how they actually use these trails. To begin with elephant shrews have large eyes and large ears, whereas in true shrews both eyes and ears are small. So we can say they have good sight and good hearing. The very long whiskers on the snout are a sure sign, if we judge from what is known about other long-whiskered animals, of a very delicate sense of touch. They could be used for feeling the way through grass or other tangled plants or in the dark, or they could be used for picking up vibrations in the air. It is possible that that is what shrews are doing when they hold their snouts up and twitch them.

An elephant shrew's trail may run for hundreds of yards. All along it will be bolt-holes into which the shrew will dive to hide itself or get its breath back when being chased. Although bounding along at top speed it seems always to know exactly where these bolt-holes are, just as it knows precisely where to put its feet down.

We cannot look into the animal's brain or see what sense it is using at a particular moment. What we can imagine, as we watch it bounding along at high speed, almost like a bouncing rubber ball, is that every sense is on the alert, and that the shrew remembers every little detail all along each trail.

69

There are Ghosts in the Tree Tops

The aye-aye is an odd-looking animal living on the island of Madagascar, off eastern Africa. It is odd enough to have made the people of Madagascar afraid of it. They believed that if it no more than touched one of them that person would die. They also believed the spirits of their ancestors lived in the aye-ayes. So if one of these animals went near a village either somebody killed it or all the villagers moved out and went to live somewhere else.

None of this is really surprising. The aye-aye sleeps by day high up in the tall forest trees, in one of several nests it builds out of sticks and leaves. It is about the size of a household cat but with a bushy tail, is black and black is associated with evil.

Dr J J Petter

Also, it has large staring eyes and large ears. Its fingers and toes are long and spooky-looking, especially the middle finger on each hand which is very long indeed. Since it only comes out at night it is easy to see how eerie it must look in the dark or even in the half-light. Its call of *aye-aye* from which it gets its name, made high up in the trees at night, sounds like two pieces of ghostly metal being rubbed together.

The aye-aye also fooled the scientists at first. They thought it was some kind of squirrel. This was because of its bushy tail and because it has two incisors (front teeth) in both upper and lower jaws, just like a squirrel. These also grow continuously at the roots as in squirrels and other rodents. The aye-aye is like a rodent in having no canine teeth. Instead, there is a gap between the incisors and the cheek teeth. In the end the scientists decided the aye-aye was a lemur, one of the several kinds related to monkeys and found only on Madagascar.

If the aye-aye is strange to look at, its habits are even more strange. It feeds mainly on insect grubs living in wood. It finds these partly by smell and partly by listening with its very sensitive ears. For a long time it has been said that the aye-aye taps the wood with one of its long middle fingers and listens, with the skill of a piano-tuner, for the change in tone indicating that there is a hollow tunnel in the wood with a grub in it. There is now some doubt about this.

Whatever the truth, once the animal has located a grub it rapidly gnaws away the wood, then pushes its long finger into the tunnel to hook out the grub. The aye-aye puts the grub into its mouth through the

Left. It is easy to see why people are frightened by the strange aye-aye. Its eyes glow in the darkness and make it look quite ghostly amid the trees.

Right. Aye-ayes lurk in the tree tops and are rarely seen as they come out at night. The drawing shows the shape of their strange hands that they use to hook out grub's from under a tree's bark.

gap between its incisors and cheek teeth. Sometimes it eats fruit, gnawing away the skin or the shell and hooking out pieces of pulp with its long finger in the same way. If there is a grub in the fruit it takes that too. It drinks by dipping its long finger in water and passing drops through the gap at a rate of 40 strokes a minute.

Aye-ayes are very difficult to observe as they only come out at night. Even with a torch it is hard to see them because of their dark colour and because they live high up in the trees. All you see is the glow of their two eyes. They are not easy to keep in captivity, and they have seldom been photographed. Almost all the photographs taken show only two points of light, the eyes, against a black background. So little else is known about this strange and rare animal except that the mother carries her one baby on her back.

Whether we shall ever know more about them is anyone's guess. Indeed, the aye-aye was thought to be extinct in 1933. Then it was seen again in 1957 and in 1966 it was thought there were less than a dozen still living. There are probably a few more than that, perhaps 50, but the rain-forest that forms their home is steadily being destroyed so that the land can be used for growing crops.

The Malagasy, as the people of Madagascar are called, are now learning not to fear it. This is partly because they are better educated and partly because they seldom see an aye-aye now, because it is almost extinct. Whether the aye-aye can be saved only time will tell.

Nine of the remaining fifty are now on an island, Nossi Mangabe, just off the northern tip of Madagascar, where there is a good rain-forest and very few people. The World Wildlife Fund paid for these to be caught and taken to Nossi Mangabe, which is now a nature reserve. The hope is that they will settle down there and breed. If they do the species will have been saved.

Dr J J Petter

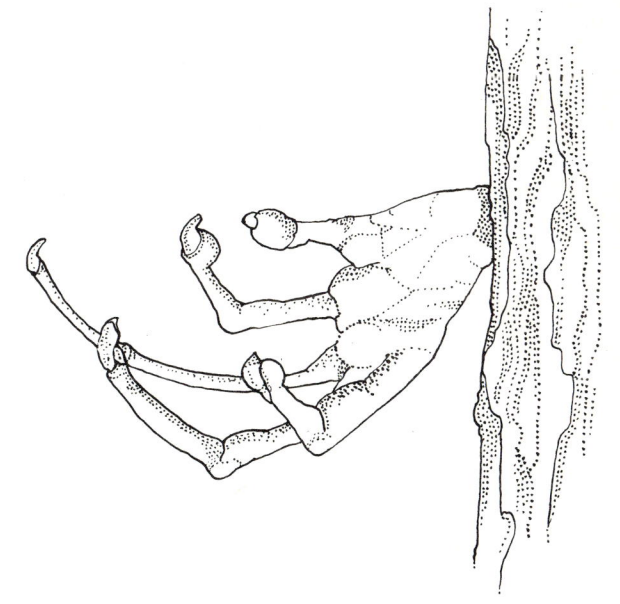

Playtime in the Sea

Several young people who have read last year's *World of Nature* have asked me about dolphins playing. They had read what I had written about the dolphin that played with bathers off the New Zealand coast, and they had seen dolphins playing in a seaquarium. One of my questioners was puzzled to know what it was sailors had seen at sea when they talked about dolphins playing.

Probably ever since men went to sea in their first crude little boats the dolphins have played around them. Then as they built larger ships they noticed that dolphins were playing in the bowwave made by the ship. But there is much more to it than this and one wonders how often sailors have seen the kind of thing which somebody wrote about 40 or 50 years ago when something like 10,000 dolphins were seen in one place in the Indian Ocean, stretched as far as the eye could see in any direction, and apparently all at play. Unfortunately we know little more about it than this.

Dolphins have an exceptional sense of fun. They leap out of the water in sheer joy, roll over and splash and smack the water with their tails, delighting in the noise this makes. A favourite sport is to leap and swim in formation, five or more dolphins together in a perfect line.

In 1956 I was on holiday on the coast of Cornwall near Land's End. Whenever I am near the sea or at sea I keep a sharp watch for dolphins or porpoises and have many times seen them swimming by arching their backs out of the water or riding in the bow-wave of a ship, but I have never seen them do anything that I would call playing. When we first arrived at Cornwall that year I was told by another visitor how he had seen dolphins playing in the bay the week before. He was most enthusiastic about the extra-ordinary spectacle that the dolphins had provided him with that week.

I could hardly believe that the same thing could happen again so quickly, yet one evening looking out of the window I saw a school of dolphins coming in from the Atlantic. They seemed to be heading for this same bay. Moreover, one of the leading dolphins suddenly leapt out of the water and came down again with a belly smacker throwing a huge wave to either side of itself. Looking back now, I think this must have been some sort of signal to the rest because they all turned and made straight for the bay where they had been seen playing a week before. As you can imagine, I lost no time in going to the top of the cliffs over-looking this bay. By the time I had got there the school of dolphins, numbering perhaps 30 to 40, had already reached the bay and were milling around so fast that it was almost impossible to count them without losing sight of what they were actually doing. And it was what they were doing that interested me more than how many dolphins were there.

The sea was quite calm and smooth and looking down from the 100 foot cliff-top we could see everything that was going on both at the surface and under the surface. How long the dolphins were playing is impossible to say now. It may have been ten minutes or a quarter of an hour that we watched spell-bound. I was trying to memorize the details of everything that was going on. It was difficult to keep one's eye on more than one dolphin at a time to be sure exactly what they were doing. What I could be sure of is that they were all milling about in the water and every now and then leaping up in the air, either in a shallow jump that carried them up through the air and back into a dive, or straight up to a height of about ten feet. Sometimes one would leap up obliquely and give a twist, then fall back into the water with a tremendous splash. It seemed not to matter whether they fell back to the water on their side, back or belly, but which-ever it was there was always a tremendous smack when they hit the water which cas-caded either side of them. Some were rolling in the water, others were jumping out and rolling before falling back into the water. At one time I noticed a dolphin standing on its head with the tail held vertically above the surface and it held this position for quite a time, standing on its head in the water so to speak. At the same time nearby another one was standing on its tail with just head and shoulders out of the water. From time to time one of them would swim at the sur-face raising its tail slowly and bringing it down with a loud smack on the water and it would do this ten times or more in succes-sion with intervals of between two to four seconds between each smack.

These are only some of the actions we saw. Looking down into the crystal clear water we could see other dolphins swim-ming about below the surface twisting and writhing but never colliding with each other. Sometimes one would swim on its back for a fair distance, either well below the surface or actually at the surface. At one moment four of them came together in line side by side and swam forward holding this formation, as if they had done so at a word of command. They swam half out of the water and half in.

The scene reminded me very much of a large bathing pool with a lot of young people in it getting up to all sorts of pranks and having a thoroughly good time. It is difficult to believe that the dolphins were not doing this for the sheer fun of it. We may go further and say that for the moment they were treating this piece of sea as a play-ground. The show ended as suddenly as it began and the dolphins streamed off in the opposite direction from which they had come and we watched them until they were well out at sea and out of sight.

Cleanliness, a Matter of Life or Death

Cleanliness is next to godliness, we are told, but sometimes, especially when we are young, we prefer to be wicked and warm. If we think keeping ourselves clean is something peculiar to human beings, then we are mistaken. The furred animals, or mammals, those most closely related to us, keep clean either by bathing or by grooming or both. When a mammal cleans its fur we call it grooming, as when a cat licks its fur. It is true that whales do not groom but they are always bathing. Birds keep their feathers clean and in good trim by bathing and, most of all, by preening. If you were able to follow a bird around all day to watch it you would be surprised how much preening it does. It must do so because its feathers are so important to it for flying that it must keep them in good condition all the time. But most birds like to get under cover to do this, otherwise an enemy might take them off their guard. So we usually see little of their toilet.

Preening is a bird's way of tidying up its feathers. If you take a quill feather, that is one of the main feathers in the wing or

Twisted into rather elegant contortions a mallard carefully preens each feather.

the tail, and, while holding the quill itself in one hand, you pass the thumb and finger of the other hand down the feather from top to bottom, you can completely disarrange the feather. If now you pass your thumb and finger from the base of the feather to the tip you find that in some extraordinary way the feather is again back to its original tidy shape. This is because the separate parts of the feather have rows of tiny hooks which act almost as zip fasteners binding each one

A marmalade cat stretches out to give its soft, dense fur a thorough clean.

to its neighbour. When you run your thumb and finger from the top downwards you are undoing the zips and pushing the parts of the feather away from each other and when you run your fingers in the opposite direction you are zipping them all together again. When a bird is preening it runs its feathers through its bill taking care to do so in the right direction. So that any feathers that have become disordered are smoothed back into shape. There is more to it than this however. At the base of the bird's tail is an oil gland. By pressing this with its bill a bird makes oil ooze out. This is known as preen oil. By getting some of this into its

75

bill before running the feathers through its bill, the bird both straightens and oils the feathers at the same time. So as you watch a bird preening you see it apparently nibbling at its tail then running one feather after another through the bill, then nibbling the tail again to get more oil into the bill and straightening another lot of feathers after this. So it goes on until all the feathers on its body have been put right.

Reptiles, frogs and toads need not be so fastidious because every so often they shed the whole of their skin. This is known as sloughing, and when an old skin is sloughed the clean, bright new skin beneath is exposed. Most of the other animals cast their outer skin. The skin of a fish is being worn away and replaced all the time. Crabs and lobsters also shed their shells from time to time. A few animals have ingenious ways of keeping clean. Starfishes and sea-urchins have tiny pincers scattered over their bodies which pick off small particles that settle on them. Some sea-anemones living where the

A young bushbuck antelope cleans her fluffy coat; adults have much smoother coats.

sandy sea-bed is stirred up by surf become covered with sand grains but they can brush themselves free of the sand. On their skins are minute hairs of protoplasm, known as cilia, that are constantly beating in time with each other. This moves the sand grains outwards and over the edge of the plate-like upper surface of the anemone. It is almost a brushing action.

Perhaps the one kind of animal we see most often cleaning themselves are the insects, such as flies and bees. Their toilet is limited but very important to them. The part of their body that must be kept clean is the antennae. If we watch an ant, for example, we soon see how important the antennae are and the same goes more or less for all insects. The antennae are usually called feelers and insects tap with them as if feeling their surroundings. But they do much more than this. The antennae are crowded with tiny sense cells, of taste and smell. These sense cells are extremely delicate and would soon go out of action if not kept spotlessly clean. This the insects do by passing their antennae through their forefeet which have special combs on them for brushing off even the most tiny particles of dirt. If the antennae were covered with dust they would be no more use to an insect than a dog's nose would be if its nostrils were blocked with cottonwool.

From all these different examples we can see why animals spend so much time cleaning themselves. For them it is not so much a matter of pride but a matter of life and death that they keep their bodies clean and functioning efficiently.

A west African grasshopper cleans its antennae by combing them with a device on its legs.

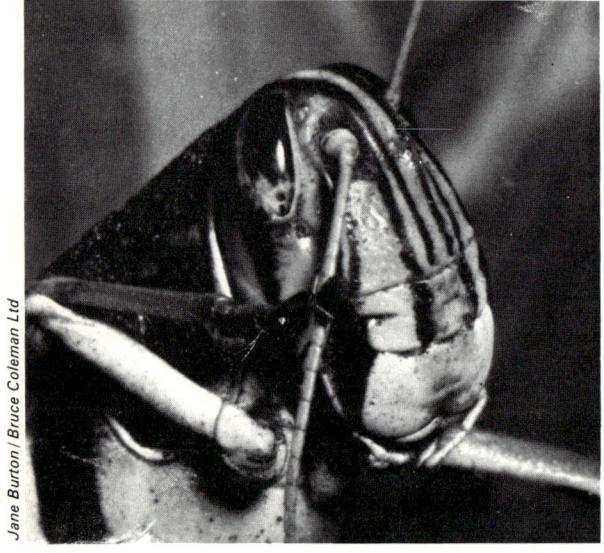

Below. Elephants play in an African river. To keep their skin in good condition they must bathe frequently, and use their trunks to squirt water all over themselves.

The small, striped fish is a cleaner fish which removes parasites from other fish, such as this flagtailed surgeon. As the cleaner feeds on the parasites and the other is kept free of pests they both benefit from their association.

Natural History Quiz Answers

1. A flock of peacocks is called a muster. This seems odd until we look into the history of the word. We are more used to speaking about mustering troops or mustering our forces, by which we mean bringing them together. The word 'muster' comes from the Latin, *monstrare*, to show. In England, in the 16th century, when roast peacock was a favourite dish at banquets, there must have been many peacocks kept. People would have been quick to notice how the peacocks were constantly displaying their trains, or showing off. In those days, to muster meant to show or display, or exhibit. In this sense it had already been used for a hundred years or more to mean bringing soldiers together, to show them off. Later it came to mean to call the roll, and then the word was used to mean bringing anything together, even to talk of mustering courage. The more widely the word became used the more its original meaning was forgotten.

2. In *Romeo and Juliet* Shakespeare wrote:

'And shrieks like mandrakes torn out of the
        earth,
    That living mortals, hearing them, run
        mad.'

And believe it or not, the mandrake, or mandragora, was only the root of a plant. There is one particular plant that is known by this name, but a number of others have also been called mandrakes, because they too have a large fleshy root that looks something like the body and legs of a human being. Centuries ago, even before Shakespeare's time, these roots had been used in making medicines. The Greeks used them to put people to sleep when they were in pain, just as today doctors give people drugs. The trouble with the mandrake was that too much caused paralysis, madness or death. The only safe way to gather the mandrake was to stuff the ears with wool because, so the legend went, it shrieked as it was pulled from the earth. Anyone hearing the shriek could die.

3. This is a very old question, one that deserves to be called a 'chestnut'. Yet it is a question that is often asked. Moreover, ask any zoologist you meet and he will almost certainly do two things. First he will laugh, secondly he will say 'I don't know'. The truth is that nobody really knows, but we have a good guide in some experiments carried out in 1938 by two American scientists.

As early as 1595, in a book called *A Thousand Wonderful Things*, we can read: 'Elephants of all other beasts do chiefly hate the mouse; so that if they should see or perceive that a mouse hath once touched their meat that is before them, they loathe the same, and will eat not a bit thereof.'

The American scientists were studying elephants and this took them to zoos and circuses. They saw that rats and mice were scurrying in and out of the bundles of hay given to the elephants to eat. It seemed to make no difference whether it was rats or mice or whether these ran over the elephants' feet. The elephants took no notice of the rats and mice.

Then the scientists thought they would try the elephants with tame white mice. It could be, they argued, that elephants used to having wild mice around might be upset at having white mice, with which they were unfamiliar. The elephants were quite unafraid of them even when they were placed on their trunks and allowed to run up and down them. Occasionally one would curl up its trunk and sniff the mice, but there was at no time any hint of alarm.

The scientists finally saw a rat scamper over a newspaper lying on the ground. This upset the elephants who became restless and trumpeted loudly. So it seems that elephants are not afraid of mice, only of the noises they make.

4. When we speak of a pit viper perhaps our first thought is of a snake that lives in a snake pit. The pit in this instance, however, is a tiny hole on each side of the head, lying between the eye and the nostril. A number of North American snakes have these pits, including moccasin snakes and rattlesnakes. In each pit is a sense organ, a heat detector. All animals give out a slight amount of heat, although in a cold-blooded animal, such as a lizard, the amount is very small. The pit viper can, however, detect a change in temperature as small as one five-hundredth of a degree Centigrade. We have small cells in our skin by which we can tell whether something is hot or cold when we touch it. Some pit vipers, such as rattlesnakes, have in each pit five times as many of these small cells as we have over the whole of our body.

The first scientists to study these pits thought they were a second pair of nostrils. Then one day, somebody noticed a rattlesnake home on a lighted match. If a pit viper is blindfolded it can still tell exactly where a mouse is by the heat from its body. But if the pits are plugged with cottonwool the snake can be right against the mouse and never attempt to eat it even if it is hungry.

Many animals are so coloured they are hard to see against their natural background. This helps to protect them from their enemies. It is useless against a pit viper, which can follow and seize its prey even in pitch dark.

By moving its head from side to side a pit viper can judge the size of the animal giving out the heat. This is necessary if it is not to waste its time on something too big for it to eat. So the pits serve the pit vipers almost as eyes, picking up heat rays instead of light rays.

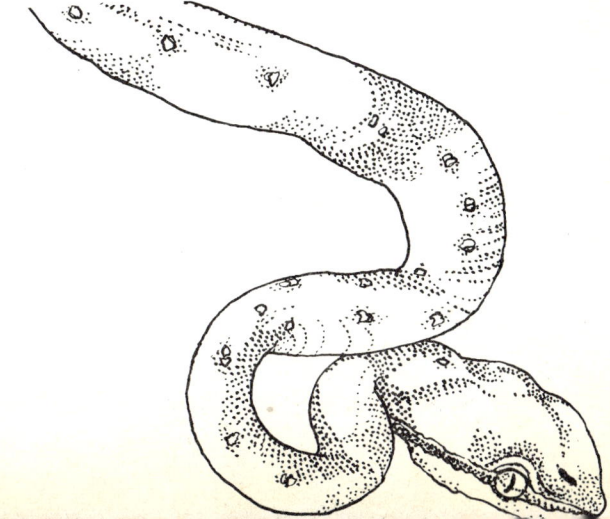

5. As you might expect, the Resurrection plant is one that seems to be quite dead but later comes to life again. The name has been given to mosses, also known as Selaginella, which close up when dry and look like birds' nests. They open up and grow green again when moistened. Another plant, the fig marigold, does something like this, and it also is sometimes called the Resurrection plant. The best known, and the one to which the name should properly be given, is the Rose of Jericho. This grows in the deserts of Israel. It is a small spreading plant of the cabbage family but its stems and roots are woody. At first it grows flat on the ground but when its seeds are ripe its branches become dry and hard and curl up and in. At the same time it loses its leaves. The seed pods remain unopened and are protected inside the skeleton-like hollow ball formed by the dry branches. So it remains until the rains come again. Then the branches un-curl, the seeds are shed and are washed out by the gushing waters.

The Rose of Jericho also spreads its seeds in another way. The plant grows in loose sand and is easily blown out by the wind and bowled along the ground. It may be blown about by the wind until it reaches a moist place, or until the rains come. Then the branches unfold and the seeds are shed.

6. If you cannot tell the difference between a pigeon and a dove there is no need to feel you are ignorant. People are often puzzled about this, and the answer is that there is no real difference. Both belong to the same family, and the use of these two names is more a matter of the history of words. The word 'dove' was from a very old word which meant something that dived. This may have referred to the way a pigeon will often fly up and then dive or glide down in a slanting flight. But that is only a guess. Anyway, 'dove' was used for all the wild pigeons native to Britain until the Normans came here. Then the Old French word 'pijon' began to be used, except for the turtle dove. With the other three species people got rather mixed up. The wood pigeon, for example, was known as the ring dove, because of its white collar. Today you seldom hear it called by that name. The tame pigeon and those we see flying about our towns are domesticated, or are descended from ancestors that were domesticated. They all came from the rock dove, which used to nest on cliffs. That is why its descendants, the tame pigeons and the town pigeons so readily take to living on buildings. There is a third species, not so well known as the other two. This is the stock dove. It often lives on sandy places and used to be called the sand pigeon.

Turtle dove.

7. In Britain as in several other parts of the world, small animals that are hard to catch are thought to be clever and intelligent. A mole-catcher, for example, will tell you how clever, cunning and artful moles are because they so often escape the traps he has set for them. In West Africa lives the water chevrotain, a kind of deer not much bigger than a domestic cat. It is hard to see, let alone catch. It lives near streams in the dense forests and is a wonderful swimmer and diver. It moves about mainly at night and takes to the water at the first sign of danger. Because of this very little is known about it but African folk-lore has it that this small deer is very, very cunning, very clever and up to all manner of tricks. The shrew is another small animal that used to be thought very clever.

Today we call a person shrewd who is clever, level-headed and long-sighted. Someone who is able to make wise judgements and who cannot be taken in. So we speak of a shrewd businessman. Surprisingly, this is what the word meant originally, in the Middle Ages. By contrast, Shakespeare uses several words that have a very different meaning. One of his plays is The Taming of the Shrew, in this instance the shrew was a sharp-tongued, ill-tempered woman. He also uses the words 'beshrew me', meaning to do harm or evil.

It seems, so far as we can judge, that this entirely different meaning began to be used towards the end of the 16th century, just before Shakespeare started to write his plays. To be shrewd then meant to be quarrelsome, bad-tempered, in fact everything that was evil.

In 16th century England people started to take a greater interest in natural history. They probably heard shrews squeaking in the grass in their high-pitched voices. They may even have heard two of them fighting over territory. They do this with a kind of squeaking match which may end by the two shrews holding each other's tails and squirming about on the ground. When they do this they make quite a noise and it is easy to see why somebody with a sharp tongue should be called shrewish or why a quarrelsome person should be called shrewd.

The people of the 16th century may, as people do today, have noticed that their cats would kill a shrew but not eat it. They got the idea that a shrew was venomous, or poisonous, and this with their high-pitched shrieks would have been enough to give birth to the idea that shrews were evil.

Hedgehog Prickles on the Sea Floor

Sea-urchins live in the sea. They are round and prickly and a large one is not much bigger than a man's fist. They have no legs but move about on hundreds of tiny suckers, known as tube-feet, helped by their spines. You can sometimes see them on the shore, especially where it is rocky. Mostly they live in deeper water. When they are moving really fast they can travel 90 feet in a day—which we can only call slow.

Our story is about a sea-urchin living in the Pacific Ocean, in fairly deep water. The first we knew about it was sixty years ago when a scientist caught a few of them in a net let down to the sea-bed where they live. Because he had caught so few he thought it must be rare. Then, a year or two ago, frogmen went down near this same spot and they saw a living carpet of them. As far as they could see in any direction were tens of thousands of this pink sea-urchin, a living carpet slowly moving over the sea-bed.

The frogmen went down to have a look at the sea-bed because the American navy had plans to put an undersea laboratory, known as Sealab III, down at that point. So came the question: What would happen with all these sea-urchins around? The scientists that would be working in the undersea laboratory would need to place instruments on the sea-bed. They would also want to set up experiments. What would happen if this living carpet moved over their laboratory and over their instruments? Would they be able to keep the sea-urchins out if they put a wire netting fence up all around?

Some of the sea-urchins were caught and brought to the surface. They were put in special aquaria so that they could be studied. The aquaria were kept in the dark, because the sea where they lived was dark. They were kept cold because the water where the sea-urchins live is cold. The sea-urchins were quite happy in the aquaria and the first thing they showed the scientists was that they could easily climb up the sides of the aquaria, holding on with their hundreds of little suckers, their tube-feet. They climbed up any pieces of wire or string hung in the aquaria. What is more, they climbed over wire-netting put in the aquaria.

Then it was found that the sea-urchins move towards a dim light. An undersea laboratory would have lights, so it would attract the sea-urchins. It would be almost as bad for the scientists working in the laboratory as it would be for a farmer trying to grow crops in a field filled with hedgehogs.

Sea-urchins usually feed on seaweeds but in deep water in the seas there is little weed for them. The scientists studied this and found they ate almost anything they came across. They are wonderful scavengers. They ate bits of dead fish or shrimps. They even ate bits of rope or plastic.

People often talk about the need to farm the seas, to provide more food for the growing populations of human beings in the world. We can begin to see from this story of the pink carpet of sea-urchins in the Pacific that the underseas farmer is going to have as many worries as the farmer growing crops on land, perhaps more.

Red and black West Indian sea urchins.

Jane Burton / Bruce Coleman Ltd

A cluster of edible West Indian sea urchins known as sea eggs.

Jane Burton / Bruce Coleman Ltd

When is a Duck not a Duck?

Food is a subject which interests nearly everyone. We all have different likes and dislikes but some things are considered to be particularly delicious by gourmets, such as oysters, venison, quail eggs and truffles.

Whether we agree with this or not people will pay a great deal of money to obtain such delicacies and often the animal or vegetable itself may become very scarce in its natural state through over-harvesting.

One such delicacy is to be had free from the beaches of the Pacific Coast of North America. That is, for people who are keen enough to work hard to dig out the animal buried in the mud.

The animal so sought after is called the go-ee-duck, but it is nothing like a duck; it is not a bird at all but a very large clam. Its name is spelt differently from how it is pronounced. When the name is written it is geoduck. Even more odd it is from a North American Indian name for the animal which sounds something like gweduck.

Clams are bivalve molluscs, which include such things as oysters and mussels. The shell is made up of two valves fastened by a hinge and a bivalve itself lives by drawing water in at one point of the shell and driving it out at another, the water bringing in food and oxygen. Clams differ from oysters and mussels in having a pair of siphons, one of which draws the water in while the other is used to drive it out again.

A peculiarity of the geoduck is that the siphons are joined, are very long and when fully stretched out are bigger than the rest of the body. When an oyster or a mussel is disturbed it can close its shells entirely to protect the soft body inside. The body of a geoduck is so large that the shell cannot close and the two valves are little more than a protective coat to part of the body.

A well-grown geoduck with its siphon fully out is about 15 inches long and will weigh about three pounds. It will then be 10 to 15 years old. Specimens weighing 8 to 10 pounds are not uncommon and the largest ever taken weighed 14 pounds. If size is anything to go by some of the geoducks must live 60 to 70 years.

The geoduck is a delicacy and practically all of its meat can be eaten, chopped up and fried, or used as steaks or ground for chowder, that is a kind of stew. It can be smoked or eaten raw and the best part is the neck or siphons.

Because it is so tasty people like to go out and dig it out of the muddy shore, but although the geoduck is a poor burrower this is not an easy task. Its burrows may be only 18 inches down but sometimes they are as deep as 7 feet. The clam lies at the bottom of its burrow and pushes its siphons up to the surface in order to take in water. As soon as the hunters get near it it pulls its siphon down and at the same time empties it of water, so giving the tell-tale jet that shows the hunters where the geoduck is. They then use their bucket, which is an open-ended 10 gallon can. This is forced into the mud until the top edge is flush with the ground. The mud inside it is then dug out, the can is pushed down again and more mud dug out, and this goes on until the geoduck can be lifted out of its burrow.

It may be hard work but that does not stop the thousands of clammers that flock to the beaches each year at low tide in the hope of capturing one or more of the clams. Indeed, their onslaughts have been such that it was feared at one time that the geoduck would become extinct. Then it was found that the geoducks living on the shore were only a tiny part of the total population.

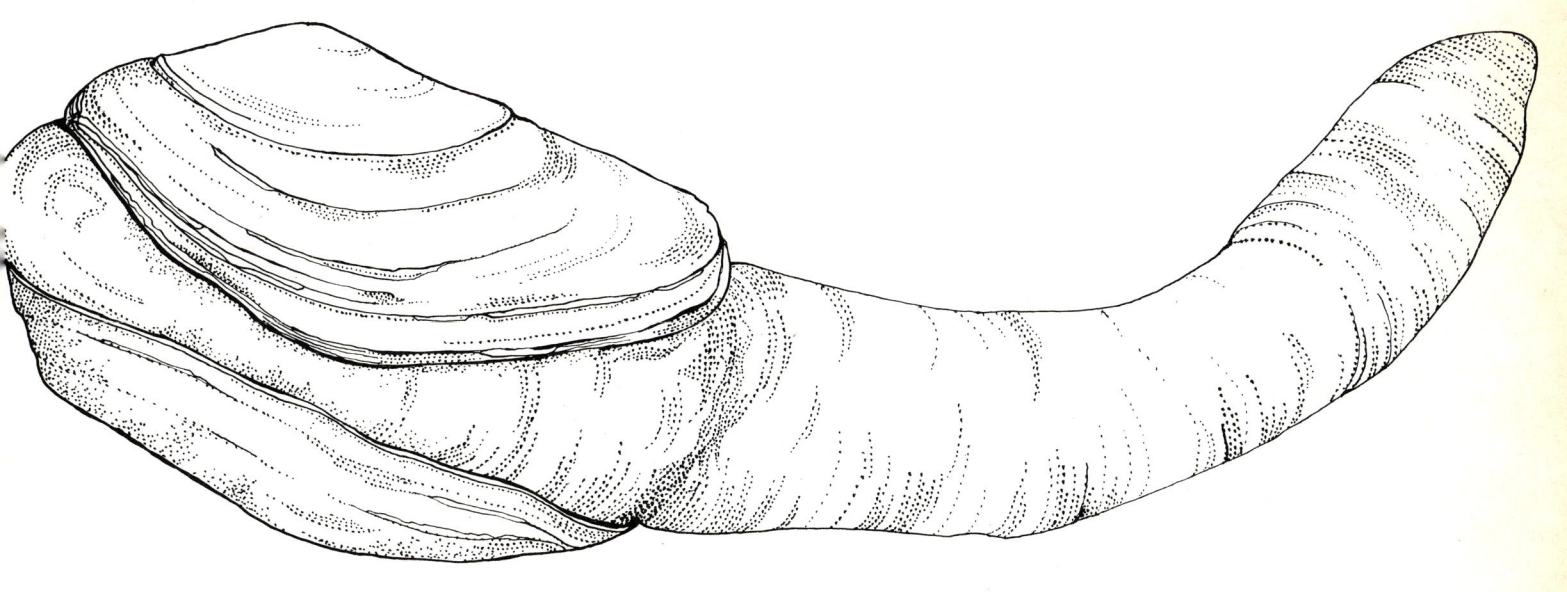

Geoducks are the largest burrowing clams in the world. They weigh as much as twelve pounds and their bodies are so big that they bulge out of their thin shells, although these are often eight inches long. The geoduck's siphon is almost as large as the body proper and stretches far enough up for the clam to live three or four feet below the muddy surface of the sea bottom. There are two siphons joined together and one is used by the geoduck to draw water and food into its body while the other expels water and waste.

Offshore, in water down to depths of 60 feet, were found tremendous numbers of them. In one small area along this coastline skin divers surveyed 15,000 acres looking for geoducks. They estimated that there were 44 million of them in this one area alone, averaging three pounds each in weight. This would mean 31,000 tons of delectable clam meat.

This number of clams could represent a fortune to somebody if only they could be easily captured. As we have seen, it is hard work digging one out from the seashore and it would be impossible even for a skin diver to dig one out under water. The only way this could be done would be by dredging. Dredging means that you use a mechanical

scoop or grab to wrench the clams from the sea bottom. Another way would be to use some kind of suction dredger. But there would be the danger that young clams would be killed and that the mud would be stirred up so that the larger ones suffered and other damage caused. In the end the beds of clams might be destroyed for ever. The United States Government therefore enacted very strict laws about how the clams could be collected. Among other things they made it a law that no clams should be taken from water less than 10 feet below low tide level. The clams living in this protected zone would produce the larvae that would settle on the shore and so make certain that there will always be geoducks for the diggers.

Beetle-Eating Flowers

On the grassy plains of East Africa grows a tree with an enormous trunk, which may be as much as thirty feet round, the baobab tree. Scattered over these same plains are acacia trees, whose leaves are eaten by giraffes. When the rains come you sometimes see, on the bare earth beneath the baobab or the acacia a pinkish something pushing its way up. At first it looks like a fungus. Then, as it pushes out more and more we see it is a flower with four thick fleshy petals that have a waxy look. This flower is most unusual and the plant on which it grows is extraordinary.

When the flower is fully opened we see it is about a foot across and is buried about nine inches in the ground. Its petals become red-looking, like a poisonous fungus. The centre of the flower is also fleshy, but yellow, quite unlike what we expect to see at the centre of a flower. There are stamens or pistils but these are hidden under the fleshy yellow ring.

The flower lasts only a day or so and its petals, which are oval at first, curl up at the edges making a partial tube. No butterflies visit this flower. Instead lots of small beetles flock to it. The largest of these is no more than a half-inch long and many are much smaller. They are the kinds of beetles that feed on dung, to which they are attracted by the smell. You would expect therefore that this flower must give out an odour of the same kind and it probably does. If so, it is one that the human nose cannot readily detect.

It is hard to find out merely by looking at the flower what this is all about. The beetles mill around under the fleshy yellow ring. The smaller of them cannot climb out and many die there. The larger beetles are able to climb out and walk over the petals.

Beetle-eating flowers grow on the plains of Africa under trees such as the acacia which provides food for this giraffe.

From there they can take off and fly away, perhaps to another of these flowers. And this is the secret.

Most plants have flowers that bear both stamens and pistils. The stamens produce the pollen. The pistils produce the seeds but not before pollen has been placed on them. In this East African plant the stamens and pistils are on separate flowers. In many flowers the pollen is carried by insects, especially bees, which are attracted to the flowers by their gay colours and their nectar. This flower attracts insects in spite of its unlovely appearance, so we may suppose, by a scent which we would call unpleasant. The important thing is that beetles are drawn to the flower to carry the pollen.

The plant producing the flower has no leaves and its stem is hard to find. It has roots and these find their way into the roots of an acacia or a baobab tree and suck food from them. So the beetle-eating plant, as it is called, although it does not really eat the beetles, is a parasite. That is, it is living at the expense of something else, battening on it, as we say. The leaves of the acacia or the baobab do the work to make the starch and sugars, so the beetle-eating plant does not need leaves. Because it is living underground it needs no stem to hold the leaves up to the sunlight so it is a plant that is little more than roots that throw up flowers in the rainy season.

There are other flowers like this in other parts of the world than East Africa. One of the more surprising of them is the one known as Rafflesia. It was named after Sir Stamford Raffles who founded the city of Singapore, in south-east Asia. Rafflesia belongs to the buttercup family, but anything less like a buttercup is hard to imagine. Like the beetle-eating flower it is a parasite on the roots of trees and it is, so far as we can tell, all root. Its flower buds push their way through the bark of the root and as the flower unfolds it pushes the earth aside. The flower buds, at first small, grow to the size of cabbages and, when fully opened, may be three feet across. The five petals on each flower are flesh-coloured with pale spots and the flower gives off an unpleasant odour to attract insects. The seeds of Rafflesia are carried about on the feet of elephants.

A close-up of the beetle-eating flower with its pink fleshy petals and yellow interior. Inside the flower are trapped a dozen or so dung beetles which scurry around the flower to try to find the way out. The beetles are attracted to the plant by its scent and if they manage to fly away will probably go to another plant taking pollen with them.

How to Help Wildlife

On December 9th, 1971, the Council of Europe Environment Campaign was launched by M. Robert Poujade, the French Minister for the Environment. Young people were enrolled as Young Nature Conservation Volunteers with a special membership card and the holders of the card pledged themselves 'to protect nature and to obey the following ten rules':

1. To respect plants and wild flowers, crops, the countryside and natural beauty spots.
2. To respect forests and to observe fire precautions meticulously.
3. To be a friend of birds and protect them.
4. To recognize the right of wild animals to live, and to protect disappearing species.
5. Not to contaminate springs, rivers, lakes or the seaside.
6. Not to scatter refuse around, but to participate in cleaning-up operations.
7. Not to disturb the silence of Nature.
8. To pay particular attention to natural reserves, and to historical and archaeological sites.
9. To enlighten those who are acting out of ignorance or error.
10. To support actively all initiatives to protect the environment.

These rules are printed here because they represent an excellent code of conduct. They do not tell us anything that we can actively do but if we have this code of conduct at the backs of our minds we are more likely to look for opportunities to carry out what they say than we would if these rules had never been put to us.

For more positive activities I have enlisted the help of a young friend, Colin Miller, aged 17 years, who is unable to lead a normal active life but is keenly interested in all natural things. He has not only put forward the suggestions but has written out what he thinks about them.

His first suggestion is that people who like to see butterflies in their garden should consider planting one or more buddleia bushes.

The buddleia bush produces a profusion of pink, mauve or purple blooms (depending on variety) from July to September. These prove an irresistible attraction to bees and butterflies, from the fritillaries to the gaily coloured peacocks, tortoiseshells, red admirals, painted ladies and the less popular whites. However, it is not so generally known that the buddleia has other uses as well. At the end of the summer, the brown, dead, rather ugly flowerheads which contain the seeds, if left on the bush until the pruning in the early spring, will provide food for several birds, notably bullfinches. Thus, to some degree, reducing their ravages in the fruit orchard. Or we can make winter decorations by picking, drying and arranging the dead flowerheads, finally spraying them with gold or copper paint. It needs only a small effort to plant a buddleia in the garden, to give a boost to the dwindling butterfly and bee populations in the summer, and help to feed some of the birds in winter.

When did you last see a frog?

Every year in March–April enormous amounts of frog spawn, together with a few adult frogs, can be seen in most ponds up and down the country. This leads one to

A group of common frog tadpoles basking on a lily leaf in a little pool of shallow water. The leaf has curled up in the sun and has stranded the tadpoles but will flatten again once the sun's rays have moved away and the tadpoles will be released back into the pond. As long as there is a little water left for them on the lily they can survive quite well in the cramped conditions unless the sun becomes extremely hot and causes them to die.

believe that frogs are still very common, but this is not so. The belief is furthered by the fact that we still call our most widespread frog the common frog, and it is now anything but common. We have two other species, being both introduced: the edible frog, found in isolated colonies in the southeast, and the marsh frog found principally on Romney Marsh.

Although the common frog lays approximately 2,000 eggs each spring, normally only about four of these will develop into adults, even under the best circumstances. Now, with increased pressures, the survival rate must have been considerably lessened. These pressures are: the filling in of ponds for building or agricultural purposes and the depositing of agricultural chemicals in ponds bordering farmland, killing the plant life and making the pond unsuitable for frogs or other creatures. Closely allied to

this is the dumping of detergents and other industrial waste into water in industrial areas. Frog spawn and tadpoles are also the victims of children who either wantonly kill them or, with the best of intentions, take them home in glass jars and then abandon them in the hope that they will carry on living. This, although it has been done for a long time now is an unfortunate practice, especially as frogs are decreasing anyway.

Frogs, I believe, add charm and interest to any garden, as well as eating many garden pests, including snails and slugs. Frogs can easily be encouraged by having a small informal pool, with plenty of cover. They can then be introduced to the pool or can be left to colonize it themselves, which they very often do in a year or two.

What has been said here also applies to the declining common toad.

Sitting pretty among lesser celandine flowers is a common frog. This name is rather misleading as their breeding grounds are decreasing and the frogs are no longer common.

Rearing frogs

When the frog spawn 'season' comes round many young people are tempted to collect a whole mass of the jelly, put it in a jar, bowl or tank, and just leave the eggs to hatch and develop. Out of a hundred or so young tadpoles, only a few, if any, will develop into froglets, and usually all these die. For a start, a common mistake with tadpoles is to overcrowd them; starting with a dozen and ending with six is obviously more worthwhile than starting with 50 and ending with none. One might say that in a pond they often seem overcrowded, but they are soon thinned out by competition for food, by disease and by numerous enemies. Tadpoles of different sizes should not be kept together, as the large ones frequently eat the smaller ones. The tadpoles should be kept in a bowl, tank or anything else with a large surface area. The water, preferably pond-water, ought to be kept quite shallow, about 2–3 inches deep, and can be replenished from time to time. The water now needs the addition of some pondweed.

At first, the tadpoles will eat algae and other microscopic plant material growing on water plants and the side of the tank. When they become more active you will know that it is time to start giving them raw meat or a chopped earthworm diet. It is best to suspend this food in the water on a length of cotton so that the remains can be pulled out after a few hours. In this way it will not turn the water putrid. Some people say that it is best to give the tadpoles live food, such as daphnia and mosquito larva, at this stage, but I have never met with much success.

The difficult stage is reached when the tadpoles have grown all four legs and are nearly frogs, for they become more active, needing more food, and it has to be live. They will take daphnia and mosquito larvæ in the water, and fruitflies, aphids and tiny earthworms on land, and the latter also in the water. However, feeding them in captivity often proves difficult and unsatisfactory; I think it is probably safer to release them in a sheltered ditch or on a pond bank.

Although several of these will die from enemies or hunger, a few will live and maybe thrive, and you have the satisfaction of knowing that in a small way you have helped to conserve a tiny part of our vanishing fauna, as well as having the interest of watching a frog start its life.

Helping nesting birds

Apart from providing nesting boxes there is little one can do to help birds during the nesting season. Indeed, the kindest thing to do is to leave them severely alone and let them get on with it. There is, however, one small way we can assist, and many people have done this. That is, by putting out materials that they can use to line their nest. This will save them the labour of flying around looking for it and to that degree will help towards success in their rearing a brood. Any ends of wool can be put out on the lawn in the garden or in other places where you judge that birds will be looking for nesting materials. People who own a long-haired dog and comb its coat regularly can help by putting out these hair combings. One important thing to remember is to put the wool or the hair well away from bushes or garden beds where a cat can lie hidden ready to spring out on the birds when they come down to collect it. A cat soon gets to know when birds are coming regularly to one place.

If you think birds will not notice what you have done remember the story of the bunches of fine plastic threads that used to be put on currant bushes known as Scaraweb. I have seen bullfinches who were building their nest a good 100 yards away from a group of currant bushes making regular trips to collect the threads of Scaraweb with which to line their nests. Small birds often use the silk threads from spider's webs for this purpose but apparently these bullfinches found the artificial threads just as good. It is worth knowing that they flew such a long distance to collect them because this will happen with other birds and the wool or hair that you put out for them. You do not necessarily have to think of birds nesting nearby the spot where you put the wool or hair as being the only ones to use it.

Bullfinches are extremely attractive garden birds. This male bullfinch is sitting on an apple tree which provides it with food but bullfinches are fond of seeds from many plants.

Picture Puzzle Answers

A. This cartwheel-shaped plant is actually a group of male flowers on a yew tree. Separate trees carry either male flowers or red female berries which contain seeds.

B. This may look like a face with eyes and an enigmatic smile. It is actually part of a skate, a large flattened fish. The picture shows the skate's mouth and nostrils which are on the underside of its body. This is because the skate feeds on bottom-living animals such as lobsters and crabs which it pounces on as they move about. The nostrils are on the underside because it locates prey by scent. The double row of darker markings are gill slits through which water is pumped back into the sea.

C. This mottled surface belongs to a plane tree and is a section of the bark. All the year round this tree's bark peels off in small sections and the mottled patches of yellow are exposed. Plane trees are very common in large cities as they are able to withstand the sooty atmosphere much better than most other types of tree.

D. The glistening wavy frills belong to an oarweed, a brown seaweed common on the coast of the British Isles. This particular specimen has been washed up on the beach, probably during a storm, and is actually several feet long. Normally the tough fronds are anchored to the sea floor by a strong root or holdfast, but this can be torn free in strong waves.

E. The two animals in this picture are Portuguese men o'war. The photograph shows their gas-filled floats which keep them buoyantly positioned on top of the water. The floats are fairly rigid and act as sails in the wind which blows the Portuguese man o'war along to new feeding grounds. It is not really a single animal but a large colony of four different polyps, which have different functions such as feeding or reproduction. All the polyps work together very intricately to form the jellyfish-like man o'war. This colonial animal is very dangerous as its long stinging tentacles trail as much as 40 feet below the float and can severely sting a bather nearby. The Portuguese man o'war uses this sting to paralyse fish which get caught in its tentacles to prevent them escaping before being eaten.

Cover picture acknowledgements: Elephant charging/South African Tourist Corporation; Spectacled elephant shrew/Jane Burton: Bruce Coleman Ltd; Mazarine Blue Butterfly/ MWF Tweedie; Forest Bug/MWF Tweedie; Waterbuck/South African Tourist Corporation; Sea urchin/Des Bartlett: Bruce Coleman Ltd. Back cover: Lion and lioness/South African Tourist Corporation.

ACKNOWLEDGEMENTS:
The publishers are grateful to the following for permission to reproduce their photographs:
Australian News and Information Bureau
South African Tourist Corporation
World Wildlife Fund
Printed in Italy